HOW TO
MAKE
IT IN
ADVERTISING

In advertising, not to be different is virtual suicide.

William Bernbach,
Founding partner of
Doyle Dane Bernbach

HOW TO MAKE IT IN ADVERTISING

MARK LEIGH AND MIKE LEPINE

Virgin

The contact details and courses offered by the various professional associations, institutions and colleges/universities listed in this book were correct at the time of going to press.

Salaries have been based on averages offered by agencies and recruitment consultancies from February to July 2000, with allowances for differentials between London and non-London agencies, which can be considerable. If you land yourself a job with a higher salary than indicated, well done. If you get offered a job with a salary lower than indicated, don't blame the authors!

First published in Great Britain in 2000 by
Virgin Publishing Ltd
Thames Wharf Studios
Rainville Road
London
W6 9HA

A catalogue record for this book is available from
the British Library.

ISBN 0 7535 0500 2

Designed and typeset by Roger Kohn Designs
Printed and bound in Great Britain by
Mackays of Chatham

ABOUT THE AUTHORS

Mark Leigh's first job in an ad agency was as a studio junior at DDB. He soon realised that there was more money (and marginally less tea-making) as an account executive there. Despite working with clients such as Polaroid, Volkswagen, Motorola, Volvic and Berkeley Homes, he is proud to say that he is 'ulcer-free'. His claim to fame is that he was once sick right in front of the Lyons Coffee client – yet still retained his job, if not his dignity. Mark is now a director of AMD, the country's largest property marketing consultancy, based in Chelsea. If his MD is reading this book Mark would like to point out to her that it was written entirely in his own time.

When called upon to write this biography, Mike Lepine was horrified to discover he had been in the 'advertising business' for over sixteen years. He's been an account director responsible for both business-to-business and consumer accounts – and yes, he once had a ponytail, Paul Smith suit and red braces. However, he swears that's all in the past now. Currently Mike works as a freelance copywriter with a number of different agencies. One day it may be the launch of BBC Timewatch videos, the next day national fire safety and the next hi-tech fibre optics. (He prefers to keep quiet about the days when it's sewage treatment or impotence cures.)

ACKNOWLEDGEMENTS

The authors would like to thank the following individuals and organisations for their kind co-operation and assistance in giving interviews and providing information for this book: Advertising Association, Sarah Bales, Don Beardsworth, Trevor Beattie, CAM Foundation, Cliff Carney, Terry Carter, Lee Charles, Chartered Institute of Marketing, John Choopani, Ben Cole, Lindsay Cole, Daryl d'Costa, British D&AD, Keith Davey, Victoria Davies, Kate Garrod, Paul Graham, Niall Hadden, Ben Harris, Jeremy Harris, Ben Hasler, Kimberley Hawkins, Jason Heaver, Colin Higgs, Nicki Hill, Tom Hopkins, Rupert Howell, Richard Huntington, Dingus Hussey, Institute of Direct Marketing, IPA, Institute of Sales Promotion, Gaye Landau-Leonard, Lisa Lines, London School of Printing, Annabel Lucas, Chris Macleod, Simon Manchipp, Vicki McGuire, Alison McLeod, Zoe Miller, Anne Murray-Chatterton, Simon North, Petra Osborne-Fardon, Kate Percival, Alf Rogers, Ryan Shellard, Julie Smith, Central St Martins College of Art & Design, Debbie Taylor, Richard Temple, Emma Thwaite, Bruce Vigar, Chris Watson, Katherine Wilkinson, Mike Williams, Tamarind Wilson.

On a personal note, the authors would like to thank Debbie, Polly and Barney Leigh, and Philippa and Gage Hatton-Lepine for their boundless patience (and cups of tea).

CONTENTS

FOREWORD

WHY ADVERTISING IN THE FIRST PLACE?

For some it's a rare opportunity to fuse commerce with creativity. Or art with science. Others like the chance to get involved in the creative process and to be able to communicate new ideas to people. Still others just like the opportunity to help clients achieve their business goals.

Whatever your motivation, most people who work in the industry wouldn't change their job for the world. If you're after routine and a nine-to-five working day then advertising's not for you. Yes, it's an old cliché, but every day *is* different. It's something you'll hear again and again if you ask someone why they like doing the particular job they do.

Yes, there's pressure. Yes, there's stress. But at the end of the day it's an industry that's really lively and fun to work in. It's one where you get a real buzz out of seeing the end product, whether it's a TV commercial or a press ad, with the knowledge that you were part of the creative process however small the role you played.

Good luck!

Rupert Howell
Founding Partner of HHCL
and President of the Institute
of Practitioners in Advertising

INTRODUCTION

A CAREER IN ADVERTISING

Let's be realistic. Yes, it's difficult to get a job in advertising. Not as difficult as getting a job as an astronaut, or Director General of the BBC, but difficult nonetheless. However, it's a career well worth pursuing and there are many opportunities for both graduates and non-graduates on the business and creative sides at an agency.

Don't think that a career in advertising pigeonholes you for the rest of your life, though. The many disciplines and skills that an advertising agency provides for its clients also means it's possible to use and develop these abilities outside the industry.

Of course, no agency wants to lose talent but some very successful people have started their careers in advertising agencies before going on to bigger and better things. Salman Rushdie used to be a copywriter and claims to have come up with the slogan 'Naughty. But nice' for the National Dairy Council. Other copywriters who have become successful authors include Ted Lewis (*Get Carter*), James Herbert and Fay Weldon. Peter Mayle, famous for spending *A Year in Provence,* used to run an agency in New York and before that wrote copy, being responsible for the Wonderloaf slogan 'Nice one, Cyril'. The illustrators Gray Jolliffe (*The Big Viagra Joke Book*) and Roger Hargreaves (*Mr Men*) were both art directors. Alex Ayuli was deputy creative director at BBDO and left after reaching number one as part of the band M.A.A.R.S. with 'Pump Up The Volume'. Andrew Nichol, who was creative director at the same agency, left to try his luck in Hollywood where he wrote *Gattaca* and *The Truman Show*. Even the authors of this book, who have had three number one bestsellers, started in advertising (and are still there in fact – not everyone makes a fortune from writing books).

And of course, there are hundreds of people who started off looking for a job in advertising, just like you and who have gone on to form their own successful agencies.

In the Foreword, Rupert Howell outlines some key reasons to pursue a career in advertising. There are others.

For a start, advertising is one of the rare industries that's very much a meritocracy; where hard work and talent can facilitate a rapid climb up the career ladder and where some of the most senior people are only in their 30s and 40s. One top London copywriter actually got his big break after writing a review of an agency football match which was pinned up on the staff notice board. At the time he was working in the production department, but his style of writing and turn of phrase caught the attention of the creative director who offered him a job as a junior copywriter. The rest, as they say, is history.

Then there's the working environment. Because essentially what they sell is creativity, agencies tend to promote themselves as being 'different' and 'original' – and this aspect is reflected in things like their décor and the way people work and dress. Want reception furniture that wouldn't look out of place in the Tate Modern? IT systems that look like art, never mind state of the art? A pool table and bar in the basement? A boss who has blue hair? You'll find them at an ad agency. (OK, very few bosses have blue hair,

but you get the picture.)

It shouldn't be overlooked that there is also the chance to make large amounts of money, particularly in a creative role. Agencies want the best talent, and are prepared to pay handsomely to recruit the people with the best, most original ideas (and pay even more to keep them there).

The one problem the industry suffers from is that it's over-glamorised as a result of cliché comedy sketches, sitcoms, and 60s films. *Take note:* these days no one looks at ad concepts and says 'Let's put it on the front porch and see if the cat licks it up' or 'Run it up the flag pole and see who salutes it'.

These clichés all added to the myth that ad agencies are full of wild and crazy people drinking far too much, having casual affairs left, right and centre, taking three-hour lunches and earning six-figure salaries for doing nothing. That might have been true 30 years ago but today the business is far more professional. The pace of the industry, driven by client demands and new technology, means that people now work far harder and are far more focused on what they do (plus of course, they never get the time for all that gallivanting).

Still interested and not tempted to take this book back and swap it for *How To Make It in Pig Farming* or *How To Make It in Occupational Health*? Good.

Let's have a look at some statistics and how you might start your career.

Most advertising agencies tend to be small businesses employing a total of around 13,000 people in the UK. There's no central register of advertising agencies, but the Institute of Practitioners in Advertising (IPA) is the industry's professional body and represents about 200 member agencies. These tend to be the larger agencies, which account for over 80% of total advertising expenditure, but there are over 500 other agencies in London alone.

As far as age and sex goes, the average age of people in the advertising industry is around 28 and although it has a reputation as a male-dominated sector, there's actually a 50:50 split, with women heading some of the largest agencies.

ATTRIBUTES FOR WORKING IN ADVERTISING

● Energy
● Passion
● Persistence
● Creativity
● Tenacity
● Diplomacy
● Being a team player
● Tolerance
● Stamina
● An interest in people and popular culture
● The ability to work quickly but accurately
● Self-motivation
● Staying cool under pressure
● Being articulate
● Not being afraid to voice your opinion
● Low blood pressure
● Blue hair
● An understanding partner who believes you when you get in at 2 a.m. and say that you were at a photographer's studio all night.

HOW DO I GET IN?

If you're a graduate, don't worry if your degree isn't related to advertising or marketing. Most graduates joining the industry don't have relevant qualifications. Since advertising is a 'people industry' most agencies are more interested in the individual, regardless of whether they have a background in law, medicine, psychology, applied mathematics, French, political studies, or even geography.

The larger agencies operate formal graduate recruitment

programmes, which are covered in a separate section (see p.19). In nearly all cases these programmes are designed to fill managerial roles such as account handling, planning or media buying.

Entry to the creative department tends to be based not on formal qualifications but on ability, which you need to demonstrate in a portfolio of your work.

People working in TV production and the creative services department, like production, traffic and the studio, tend to learn 'on the job' and some of the brightest people in these fields have started as receptionists, studio juniors, secretaries and even dispatch riders.

Some of the jobs in this book are 'entry-level' positions but we've also included some to show how you can progress within a department. It's highly unlikely, for example, that you're going to walk into an agency and get a job as creative director or TV producer. However, you can aspire to these positions.

(We've left out roles like secretary, receptionist, accountant or financial director as these are not industry-specific enough and what you'd do in an ad agency in this role is pretty much what you'd do in any company.)

In the following pages you'll learn about the different roles within an agency, although some of the titles might differ. For example, in some agencies, account managers are called account supervisors. In others, account supervisor is a separate position between account executive and account manager. There's also a blurring between the functions of an art director, a designer and an artworker; different agencies have different interpretations of what these functions are and what responsibilities they have.

However, whatever your title, the basic principles of each job apply, no matter what the size of the company you work for. There will be people thinking up the ads, people producing them, people liaising with the clients and people booking the space. The larger the agency, the more defined the roles will be, so it's likely you will have a separate art buyer, production and traffic person. Smaller agencies will tend to combine these roles and in some companies you might find that the account handlers also deal with a bit of production or even copywriting.

Whatever your career interests, what's vital to remember is that each person, at whatever level or in whatever role, is an integral part of a team and only through good teamwork can the best advertising be created.

Today, the growing number of magazines, the proliferation of TV channels and the relevance of the Internet to all aspects of our lives makes it one of the most exciting times to work in advertising. The public are far more sophisticated when it comes to design, and far more cynical when it comes to communications. What this means is that advertising needs to be more creative, more hard hitting and more integrated across all forms of media in order to present one cohesive, co-ordinated and credible message.

Now if that's not a challenge, what is!

Mark Leigh and
Mike Lepine
(neither of whom has blue hair)

TYPES OF AGENCY

You'd be forgiven for thinking that there were only about twenty ad agencies in the UK. That's because the ones that end up in the public eye have a very high profile due to the work they're producing, the clients they work for and the flamboyant personalities of some of the key people.

A lot of the work they produce is for clients in the FMCG (Fast Moving Consumer Goods) sector which, as its name suggests, involves products that people consume. Fast. This includes anything from Mars bars to microwavable pizzas, baked beans to bottled water. The nature of these products means that TV advertising is often used to reach a large audience – which in turn means that more people see the commercials, and talk about them, which sometimes generates publicity about the commercial itself. (Cases in point are the Wonderbra posters and the Tango TV commercials. And who can forget *Fly Fishing* by J R Hartley?)

HHCL, JWT, BMP DDB, M&C Saatchi, TBWA, Leagas Delaney, BBH, WCRS, McCann-Erickson, CDP, Leo Burnett, Publicis, AMV and Ogilvy & Mather. None of these agencies are really household names (or initials), but you'll see them in the general news now and again. It's true that they're among the largest and most successful, but for every JWT there are literally hundreds of smaller agencies not just in London but in most major cities and towns.

The size and the client list of these agencies means it's unlikely you would have heard of them. Unlike the large agencies, who work predominantly with high-profile consumer clients, many smaller agencies specialise in particular markets, creating a niche for themselves. These include agencies that specialise in advertising property, high-tech products, building materials, aviation products, computer games, industrial products, fashion, music – and many other specific market sectors.

One phrase you'll see cropping up again and again is 'Full Service Agency'. This basically means that the agency offers account management, planning, creative work, studio facilities, media buying and even sometimes public relations all under one roof (or through affiliated companies if not physically under one roof). Some agencies will provide everything in-house, but will use a separate media specialist to plan and book media (called a media independent). Others might offer all the services apart from planning, and use freelance planners as and when required. It all comes down to the structure of the agency, its size, its culture and its history.

There are also the following specialist types of advertising agencies. Some of these will be independent agencies in their own right; others will be specialist divisions of an established agency network.

BUSINESS-TO-BUSINESS AGENCIES

These specialise in promoting products and services not to the public, but to other businesses, organisations or specialist professionals. For example, a company that manufactures bricks would promote them to the architect; a company that manufactures buses would promote them to the companies that run bus services.

In practice there's no difference between the way business-to-business agencies and consumer-orientated agencies are structured and run. It's just the target audiences that are different.

RECRUITMENT AGENCIES

Here the advertising is solely designed to find people to fill job vacancies. Recruitment agencies often provide additional services such as screening candidates.

HEALTHCARE AGENCIES

These agencies work on behalf of pharmaceutical clients, promoting drugs and medicines to doctors and other healthcare professionals. Don't worry. You don't need to be a pharmacist or a junior doctor to work here. These agencies have access to a wide range of professional consultants who advise them on issues like the strict legal guidelines that govern what can and can't be claimed in this field.

DIRECT MARKETING (DM) AGENCIES

While advertising *per se* is designed to build awareness of brands or products across a wide audience, direct marketing is concerned with targeting the communication to reach a specific audience, usually by using a database. This database can take many forms. It might be a list of people who made enquiries about a new car but didn't actually purchase it. It might be people living within a five-mile radius of a new supermarket. It might be people who bought life insurance from their bank but not a pension. It might be those aged 18–21, those with a dog, those who don't have double glazing, or those who don't own their own house. All of us are on hundreds of lists and direct marketing agencies can purchase these for their own use.

The most popular form of direct marketing (also called direct response) is direct mail. It's what consumers know as 'junk mail'. This is mail which is personally addressed and targeted to one specific person. If the advertiser (and their direct marketing agency) has done their homework it will involve a product or service that the recipient will be interested in. Sometimes it all goes wrong and a 75-year-old retiree will get a mailing about a new range of flavoured condoms (though this is usually the fault of the list owner, not the agency).

Other forms of direct marketing include telesales, door-to-door canvassing, leaflets dropped through your letterbox and, lately, the Internet.

Clients often use some form of direct marketing as part of their overall communications programme and specialist direct marketing agencies have grown to serve their needs. They operate in much the same way as traditional advertising agencies with creative, planning, media and account handling positions. There are also roles in analysing and interpreting response data from campaigns.

Further information about careers in Direct Marketing, opportunities for graduates and professional qualifications in the field, can be obtained from:

The Institute of Direct Marketing (IDM)
1 Park Road
TEDDINGTON
Middlesex TW11 0AR
TEL 020 8977 5705
WEBSITE www.theidm.co.uk

SALES PROMOTION AGENCIES

Sales promotion is the practice of encouraging customers to try a product or service, usually in the short term. This is achieved with the help of incentives that can take many forms. The most common are money-off coupons, on-pack competitions, free gifts inside products and coupons to collect and redeem as gifts. Since these promotions are for a limited period, the effect on sales can easily be measured.

Long-term sales promotion techniques include various loyalty card schemes, the issuing of Air Miles, and points earned when shopping at supermarkets or petrol stations. The information gleaned from these cards is often used in direct marketing (above). For example, if Tesco knows from the information on your loyalty card that you frequently buy wine, then it can mail you details of special wine promotions.

Sales promotion agencies (also called 'below the line' or BTL agencies) devise and implement these schemes and are also structured like traditional ad agencies.

Further information about careers in sales promotion and professional qualifications in this field, can be obtained from:
The Institute of Sales Promotion (ISP)
Arena House
66-68 Pentonville Road
Islington
LONDON N1 9HS
TEL 020 7837 5340
WEBSITE www.isp.org.uk

NEW MEDIA AGENCIES

There has been a recent proliferation of agencies specialising in the creation and programming of web-sites, banner advertising, e-commerce applications, advertising on WAP mobile phones and viral marketing (this is where advertising messages are passed on via e-mail – for example, the Budweiser frogs screen saver).

It's an industry that's constantly evolving. One of the latest developments is advertising on PDAs (Personal Digital Assistants, such as the Palm Pilot).

There's been a trend by large agencies to launch their own New Media divisions to cater for clients' needs in this arena. An example of one of these is Publicis Networks, owned by Publicis. Mike Williams, its managing director says, 'We established Publicis Networks to develop new media capabilities in order to serve the clients of the main agency. When you consider that these clients may spend 5–10% of their budgets on new media applications, it makes sense to keep it in house. In the time we've been going we've also developed our own clients which now account for about 40% of our work. We offer clients integrated thinking but, unlike a lot of new media agencies, we're objective when it comes to the brief. If a client asks us for a new website we ask "why?". Sometimes they don't actually need one. It may be a different marketing tool that will meet their needs, one that another of the Publicis group companies might provide. It's all a question of balancing our business needs and objectives with customer solutions and thinking in a media-neutral way.'

Of late, a number of smaller new media divisions have been sold back to their original owners or absorbed into the main agency as they weren't as financially viable as first thought. That said, it's an area that's still growing and provides opportunities for programmers, designers and account handlers. (See **New Media Opportunities**.)

Revolution magazine is a useful publication for job opportunities in this sector:

WEBSITE
www.revolution.haynet.com
SUBSCRIPTION DETAILS
020 8841 3970

AGENCIES OUTSIDE LONDON

Competition for jobs is less fierce in agencies outside London. Some of these companies are subsidiaries of the large London agencies, such as BDH TBWA, JWT Manchester and McCann-Erickson Manchester. Others are independent agencies in their own right with a good reputation for creativity, such as the Poulter Partnership in Leeds and The Leith agency, 1576 Advertising and Faulds Advertising in Edinburgh.

You can find a list of regional advertising agencies in the Yearbook published by the magazine **Adline**.

Contact:

Adline Publishing Limited
Adline House
361-363 Moseley Road
BIRMINGHAM B12 9DE

GRADUATE TRAINING SCHEMES

● **WARNING:** If you want to work in the creative department, don't read this section. Go to **How to Get Into the Creative Department** instead (p.46).

It's no harder today to get into an agency than it was in the past. It's *always* been difficult.

Most of the large London advertising agencies offer graduate training schemes primarily for those who want a career as an account handler. Some roles such as junior planners or media planners might also be offered if an agency feels a successful candidate is more suited for this position.

These schemes are always, always, *always*, really heavily subscribed. Large agencies receive about 2000 to 3500 applications for every five positions they need to fill. If you're successful you'll probably be offered a job in January and will start work the following September.

If you want a job on the creative side, then these schemes aren't for you. And don't even think about pretending you want a job as a junior account executive just to get a foot in the door so you can suddenly rip off your account executive mask and say, 'Ta-da! I really want to be a copywriter.' (In any case, you'll be sussed out long before this.)

If you're interested in joining one of these Graduate Training Schemes, then the IPA (Institute of Practitioners in Advertising) issues a 'Graduate Fact File' at the beginning of October each year. This gives details of all its member agencies that are offering Graduate Training Schemes that year. If you don't obtain a copy of this, you'll have to contact the agencies directly to see if they offer a scheme. If they do, then request an application form and find out when these have to be sent back (they tend to be issued in the autumn).

It doesn't matter if you apply to more than one agency. You'd be daft if you didn't and agencies expect you to. However, what's vital is making sure that you really understand the individual companies you approach.

Agencies, like people, have different personalities. Some are very cool and trendy so if they ask for a photo, you might consider sending one showing your blue hair. Others are more formal so this would be a definite no-no. Some pride themselves on being radical in their approach to advertising and some place more importance on achieving quantifiable results for clients.

Before you decide which company you would like to work for, make sure you understand these differences. Read *Campaign* magazine (the ad industry's weekly magazine, published every Thursday) so you can keep up with their account wins and losses. *Marketing Week* and *Marketing* (both published on Wednesday) also have news sections on advertising. Most of the large agencies have good websites so check them out. You can always phone an agency's reception and ask for a client list, explaining why you want it. The *Guardian*, *Telegraph*, *London Evening Standard*, *Independent* and *The Times* all run media columns so keep an eye out for these as well.

The Advertising Association in London SW1 has a library with information on ad agencies, but visits are by appointment only. Call 020 7828 2771.

Learn about the agency's clients, how the company is structured, its size, its growth and even its philosophy (if it has one). Only by gathering this information will you be able to assess each of the companies you're interested in and see if they meet your ideals and your aspirations. This will help you avoid being shortlisted for a job at an agency that works for the Meat Marketing Board, the Turkish Secret Police, Marlboro, the Royal Navy and the Association of Abattoirs if you're a committed vegetarian, pacifist and non-smoker.

(Incidentally, most large agencies handle cigarette advertising in one form or another. And if not, then they probably advertise brands owned by tobacco companies, so any morals might have to be put on hold if you really want a job at a top agency.)

Zoe Miller is PA to the Managing Director of M&C Saatchi and co-ordinates the agency's graduate recruitment and training scheme with her colleague Victoria Davies, an account director on British Airways.

M&C Saatchi take on four or five graduates a year through their graduate recruitment scheme, one for each of their account-handling groups, which is about average for an agency of its size (250 staff).

Zoe and Victoria say, 'Each September we send out about 2000 application forms to interested graduates. These have to be returned to us by mid-November together with a one-sided CV and a brief covering letter. We usually get about 800 application forms back.

'We spend a lot of time each year creating the form. It usually has four questions designed to ascertain the following:

1 Creative ability
2 Ability to sell/persuade
3 Understanding of the advertising process
4 Personality

'While there is no magic answer to any of the questions, an abiding agency principle is the "Brutal Simplicity of Thought", based on the belief that it is easier to complicate than to simplify. Therefore, we ask candidates to keep their answers brutally simple.

'Education and qualifications are one part of our consideration. We're looking for people who are right for the agency, and in most cases they happen to be graduates. We have, in the past, hired trainee account executives that are not graduates, but via other routes such as the work placement scheme.

'After the closing date we assess the applications with a selection of group account directors, senior account directors and planners and from the shortlist we invite about 100–120 applicants for a first-round interview.

'The first-round interviews take place in the agency in December over three days, each interview lasting for half an hour. Each candidate spends fifteen minutes with a group account director and fifteen minutes with an account director. They will be shown different ads to get their reactions and views as well as a more general interview to assess their personality and understanding of the role of an account manager.

'From this initial group we ask 20–25 back for second-round interviews. These take place in the agency in January and last for a whole day.

'The day usually starts with a presentation over breakfast from our joint chief executives, introducing the agency and our creative work. Candidates then break into syndicate work groups undertaking different tasks such as debates, problem solving and a mini presentation that they each come prepared with.

'There is time over lunch for candidates to meet with our account executives to talk about the job and have a tour of the agency. Then in the afternoon each group is given a creative brief to work on, from which they are asked to come up with a strategy, media proposals and initial creative concepts for a brand that they later present to their interviewers and the other syndicate groups.

'We finish the day with a more social 'getting to know you' evening with drinks and dinner.

'Successful candidates will be offered a job in account management starting the following September. Occasionally we might hire a junior account planner through this route.

'If someone was interested in a career in advertising we would advise them to find out as much as they could about all the agencies, to concentrate on those they really want to work for, to enjoy the interviews, to be persistent and stick at it.'

THE APPLICATION FORM

Applying for a place on an agency graduate training scheme isn't like applying for a passport. Or a resident's parking permit. Or a job at McDonalds. The first thing you'll notice is that the application form itself sometimes isn't actually a form. In most cases it is, but some agencies, conscious of the fact that they need to create something that sets them apart and reflects their personality, do something quite different.

An application form for Saatchi and Saatchi once included a roll of film and asked applicants to take photos of themselves, a location of their choice and something that annoyed them – writing 100 words on each subject.

Another application form from the same agency was actually an empty envelope in which candidates had to send a variety of things back. These included a postcard telling the agency about an important journey they once made and something that represented the candidate – a visual metaphor, if you like – explaining its relevance.

Other agencies are just as innovative when it comes to what the applicants receive but even if the form itself is conventional, you can be sure that the questions it asks will not be.

Application forms have included things like:

● Write an advertisement to promote fire, or the wheel, to someone who's never heard of the concepts.

● Sell yourself to us in an advertisement using a three-word headline and 30 words of copy.

● What cause do you really feel passionate about? Devise your own TV commercial to promote this cause.

● What would you do if you were asked to work on a campaign designed to promote whisky to teenagers?

● Write a slogan of not more than eight words which sums you up.

● What is the worst thing that could ever happen to you, and why?

● You are working on a pitch for new business when you accidentally receive a copy of one of your rival's presentations two days before. Would you use it to your advantage?

● Who is the most creative person you know, and why?

● Which person has been the greatest influence in your life and why?

● If we offered you a three-month sabbatical after five years, what would you do with the time?

● Which character from history would you have liked to be, and why?

● Write three headlines for an ad that promotes a perfume or aftershave that makes you irresistible to the opposite sex (the product has been scientifically proven).

● Which is the worst advertisement or commercial you have seen, and why?

Tricky, eh? That's because these application forms serve two purposes. The first is obviously to find out about you – how you think and what sort of personality you have. The second reason is that by making them difficult and very time consuming, they act as a sort of filter for anyone who's not that serious about applying.

If you are serious, and you're really committed towards a job in advertising, then you'll enjoy having to think and be creative before filling them out.

TIPS FOR COMPLETING APPLICATION FORMS

Remember that, unless you get shortlisted for an interview, these forms will be your only contact with the agency. They have to speak for you and represent you, which is why presentation is everything. But apart from making sure they're legible and correct in terms of spelling, grammar and punctuation, follow these tips:

● Really consider your answers. It's a cliché – and a headline that's probably been used in several thousand advertisements – but *you never get a second chance to make a first impression.*

● Draft several responses and work on these before finalising exactly what you're going to say.

● If a question says, 'In 150 words', write about 150 (no one is going to count them – they're not that sad). But don't think you can get away with 50 words. Or 850.

● Be original and say what you really think. There are no right or wrong answers in these application forms (well, apart from your name, age, sex and address). The agencies are looking for candidates who demonstrate above all else, intelligence and originality.

● Don't include anything that you can't backup at interview stage. For example, if you say you like the theatre, be prepared to discuss the last two plays you went to see (and don't think you can get away with discussing *The Rocky Horror Show* that you last saw two years ago).

● Don't pester an agency to see if they've received your form. If you're that worried, send it by registered post. If you call, it's highly unlikely that any person you manage to get through to will a) know, or b) care about your individual form – one of 3000 that have recently flooded into the offices. If you are successful then you'll hear about it at the allotted time.

INTERVIEWS

Many agencies follow the format outlined by Zoe Miller and Victoria Davies above.

The first interviews are quite short and informal while the second ones are far more intense and nearly always involve the candidates working on a presentation where they will need to show and discuss a creative and media strategy and samples of work. In a lot of cases these take place in the agency, but some second-interview candidates end up spending a weekend at a hotel while they're put through their paces.

This gives the agency a really good opportunity to gain a clear impression of their ability, interpersonal skills and stamina (the programme is sometimes devised so candidates have to perform after only a few hours' sleep over the whole two days).

TIPS FOR INTERVIEWS

According to which study you read, interviewers make up their minds about candidates within either ten or fifteen seconds. That means you have to look smart, intelligent, cool, calm and collected, and exude confidence, as soon as you walk through the door (that's not too much to ask, is it?).

In addition to that...

● Make sure you arrive at the right place at the right time.
● Make sure you're up-to-date with news about the agency. Wins, losses, new staff, awards won – all that sort of thing. You might not be asked about these at the interview but it doesn't hurt to drop them in at the appropriate time (as long as it doesn't look as though you're trying too hard).
● Be yourself and don't put on airs and graces to try and impress the interviewer. If you've got an accent that makes Janet Street-Porter sound like Princess Anne, then don't try and disguise it. The people you'll be talking to have seen it all before and can spot fakes a mile off.
● Make sure you feel comfortable with what you're wearing. If possible, try and find out the dress code of the agency. Loitering outside after six o'clock should give you a clue. There's no point in turning up in a three-piece suit if 'smart casual' is the order of the day.
● Even if it wasn't asked in the application form, have carefully prepared answers for a) 'Why do you want to work in advertising?' and b) 'Tell me about two ads you like and two you really hate.' It's amazing how many people haven't prepared for this last question and spend an embarrassing amount of time fidgeting, desperately trying to remember what they saw on TV the previous night.
● Always have a view on anything the interviewer asks. Replies that will not impress them are 'Dunno' and 'Not

sure'. 'Who cares?' is also not advisable. If you're critiquing ads then just be honest and objective. The interviewer is trying to ascertain the thought process you go through to arrive at an answer, rather than the answer itself.

● Don't smoke.

● Maintain eye contact.

● Make sure you come prepared with a list of questions you would like to ask the interviewer (if you get the chance). Don't ask about salaries. That's just tacky. Ask intelligent questions like, 'How important is it for the agency to win awards?' 'What's the average length of time a graduate trainee stays at your agency?' 'Do you think the calibre of graduates is rising or falling?' 'Do you have a dedicated new business resource?' – that sort of thing.

WARNING

The following incidents actually happened at interviews. Do not repeat them! (*source: Parade Magazine*)

● A candidate challenged the interviewer to arm wrestle.

● A balding candidate excused himself for a minute before returning to the room wearing a wig.

● A candidate interrupted the questioning in order to telephone her therapist for advice.

Needless to say, none of these people were short listed...

WHAT SORT OF PEOPLE ARE AGENCIES LOOKING FOR?

There's no set answer to this because it varies according to the type of agency. However, broadly speaking, agencies want people who are bright, personable and passionate. People who can act on their own initiative, who are not afraid to make decisions and who can demonstrate originality and intelligence.

What they are not looking for are people who are arrogant, self-centred, over-timid, inarticulate or domineering.

AND IF YOU DON'T GET OFFERED A JOB?

Don't worry.

OK, worry. But then pick yourself up and have another go.

Resilience is vital if you want to succeed in advertising. Aside from interviews, just in the course of a normal working day there are so many things a client can reject: budgets, briefs, strategies, media plans and, of course, creative work. Each time, you have to persevere and live to fight another day.

Not receiving that job offer or not reaching that second interview probably isn't a reflection of your abilities – otherwise you wouldn't have got so far. It's usually more a case of your not being suited to that particular agency, or to that particular role. For example, you might be more effective as a media buyer or a planner than an account person. But there are loads of other companies out there for you to try.

If someone tells you to stay in touch, then do. They usually don't say it unless they mean it. That doesn't mean pestering them. A friendly letter or phone call every other month won't do any harm and will show you are still keen.

If you've finally exhausted all your applications, but you're still as enthusiastic as ever, then why not consider an alternative way into the industry. For that, you'll have to read **Other Routes into Advertising** (p.37).

USEFUL ADDRESSES

The Institute of Practitioners in Advertising
44 Belgrave Square
LONDON SW1X 8QS
TEL 020 7235 7020
WEBSITE www.ipa.co.uk

Campaign Magazine
174 Hammersmith Road
LONDON W6 7JP
TEL 020 7413 4570
WEBSITE www.campaignlive.com

The Advertising Association
Abford House
15 Wilton Road
LONDON SW1 1NJ
TEL 020 7828 2771
WEBSITE www.adassoc.org.uk

The following advertising agencies are offering graduate recruitment programmes in 2000 (source: IPA Advertising Factfile February 2000).

FULL SERVICE AGENCIES
- Abbott Mead Vickers BBDO
- Bartle Bogle Hegarty
- BMP DDB
- A V Browne Advertising (Belfast)
- Leo Burnett
- Crammond Dickens Lerner
- D'Arcy
- EURO RSCG Wnek Gosper
- Grey Advertising
- McCann-Erickson Manchester
- Ogilvy & Mather
- Poulter Partners
- Publicis
- Rapier
- M&C Saatchi
- Target Direct Marketing
- TBWA GGT Simons Palmer
- J Walter Thompson
- WCRS

MEDIA SPECIALIST AGENCIES

- Austin West Media
- Booth Lockett Makin
- CIA Medianetwork
- The Media Shop Holdings
- Posterscope
- Walker Media Ltd

BUSINESS-TO-BUSINESS

- Elixir Marketing Communications

For a copy of the IPA's 'Graduate Careers in Advertising agencies' booklet write to:

IPA
Dept R
44 Belgrave Square
LONDON SW1X 8QS

Enclose a large stamped addressed envelope (66p)

CV TIPS

Possibly the most important advertisement you'll ever be involved with in your career, is your CV. This is the piece of paper that sells you to a potential employer. It's up to you to make the proposition and the benefits as convincing as possible. And like walking into an interview, first impressions matter. If your CV does not attract the reader's attention in the first 20–30 seconds then your chances of getting that precious interview have gone.

Most large advertising agencies are awash with unsolicited CVs. Some client services directors or MDs receive 20–30 a week from people like you trying to get a break. Unfortunately, the pressures of their normal day-to-day jobs means they don't have time to carefully consider every one and it's often the first, cursory glance which will determine whether your CV ends up in the folder marked 'Possible', or in the bin.

To help sort the wheat from the chaff it's easier for them to look for reasons why they *shouldn't* hire you. Things like misspellings of names or bad punctuation or grammar – even in the covering letter – will be enough to put them off.

It might seem unfair, unjust and unreasonable but the reason they do this is because they can. All advertising agency positions are so oversubscribed that they are able to be very, very picky even about who they consider for an interview.

The tips in this section won't guarantee you'll get an interview, but by following them, you will increase your chances whether you're after work experience or a full-time job.

ARE YOU SENDING IT TO THE RIGHT PERSON?

It sounds obvious but you'd be surprised how many people send their CVs to the wrong person. Yes, it is important to impress a chairman or chief executive but they won't have time to read your CV. Their PA will probably pass it on to the relevant person but then again, it might end up getting lost in the internal post system, or under a pile of papers on their desk.

Avoid these problems by sending your CV to the right person in the first place.

For a job in media, write to

the media director. For a job in account handling, write to the client services director. For a job in planning write to the planning director. Production, traffic or the studio? Write to the creative services director.

If you're looking for a job in the creative department then read the section **How to Get into the Creative Department**.

Call the switchboard to get the name of the right person and check, not only the spelling, but their actual job title as well. Client service directors don't like being addressed as client services managers. Media directors don't like being addressed as media planners. And no one likes being addressed as *To Whom It May Concern*. In the case of women are they Mrs, Miss or Ms? Some get easily offended if you assume they're married. Others get offended if you assume they're single. Again, if you're not sure, ring their PA or secretary and ask how they prefer to be addressed.

ENVELOPES
Some people say that sending a CV by second class post shows the agency that you're not that serious about getting a job.

Others say that if you're already in employment, you shouldn't use the company franking machine: this just indicates that you're taking advantage of your employer (all right, so it's only to the advantage of 26p). Others say don't use coloured envelopes: they might stand out in the post but it gives an impression that you're trivial. Good advice or not?

Well, in most cases the envelopes will be opened by a PA or secretary before the CV gets to the senior manager who's considering it. That means it's irrelevant what it looks like or what value stamp it has on it. However, it's probably better to play safe and go for a plain white A4 envelope (preferably with a stiff card insert) with a typed label and a first class stamp on it.

The reason you should go for a stiffened A4 envelope is to make sure the CV arrives flat and therefore instantly more presentable.

PRESENTATION
Although in advertising a good idea is a good idea, if it's presented properly there's a better chance of its being sold to a client. And the same goes for CVs.

Alison McLeod is Managing Director of Talisman, a large recruitment consultancy. She offers this advice:

'CVs should be no more than two pages of A4 and always on crisp, white paper. Don't be clever and try out loads of fonts. Use one that's clear and easily readable. You should put your name on the top and a box containing your key characteristics just below this. Employment and educational qualifications should then be listed in reverse chronological order. Use bullet points to highlight what you achieved at each job and what your responsibilities were. Remember to give a brief description of each company you've worked for, even if it was temporary holiday employment. Don't assume that everyone else would have heard of them. When it comes to the tone of your CV, don't make it too clever or too witty.'

Most people have colour printers at home. If you want to enhance the look of your CV, use colour conservatively, probably only for highlighting headings. You want to come across as someone who's professional – not someone who doesn't care how much ink jet cartridges cost.

CONTENT
It's important that the CV is laid out clearly, concisely and logically. The usual order is:

● Name, contact details and a brief description of your character
● Your objectives or goals (optional)
● Education and qualifications
● Work experience or employment
● Achievements
● Skills
● Interests
● References
● Personal details (some people prefer to put this information at the top of the first page)

Although *Curriculum Vitae* is Latin for 'life story', there's really no need to write more than two sides of A4. Remember, recruiters are looking for a general idea of your education, skills and personality. You can expand on the detail at the interview.

Oh yes, always send a top copy, never a photocopy.

NAME, CONTACT DETAILS AND CHARACTER SUMMARY
List your home, work (if relevant) and mobile telephone numbers. Most people

nowadays also list their e-mail address as a matter of course. If you're still studying, list your home and term-time contact details.

In terms of character traits, try and sum yourself up in half a dozen key words. There are certain characteristics that employers are looking for: motivated, organised, innovative, a team player, self-starter, conscientious, creative, inventive, dedicated, principled. (They do not favour these words: belligerent, lazy, dishonest, disruptive, incontinent or thick.)

OBJECTIVES OR GOALS

Not many people use these headings on their CV, although they can be a useful differentiator if written well. Things like, 'a career in media planning' and 'to be involved in the process of innovative and effective advertising' are succinct and uncontentious. 'Doing your job by the time I'm 25' or 'making a fortune' are trite and not likely to impress whoever is reading your CV.

EDUCATION AND QUALIFICATIONS

Your most recent qualifications should come first. Degrees and A-levels should be listed with grades, but GCSEs can be listed as 'GCSE passes in these subjects' – then list them.

The title and a summary of your project, thesis or dissertation (if you had one) should also be given.

Qualifications should also include language or computer skills you've mastered (if you're proficient in something like Microsoft Publisher but don't have a formal qualification in it, then list this under 'Skills').

WORK EXPERIENCE OR EMPLOYMENT

Again, start with the most recent jobs you've had, listing the employer first, a brief description of the company, the dates of employment and then the position. Even if you only spent two days at a relevant company doing work experience, include this. List your main responsibilities for each job.

If you took time out to travel or whatever, then give details for this period as well. Large gaps in your CV look suspicious. For all the employer knows, those missing three months in 1997 might have been due to your spending time in rehab, prison or a coma.

ACHIEVEMENTS

These should give the recruiter an indication of your character and demonstrate traits like resilience, initiative, compassion, creativity, leadership, working under pressure or to deadlines – that sort of thing.

Even information like playing in a band, promoting yourselves and bringing out a CD is useful. It shows you as a team player and demonstrates your taking the initiative and doing something creative (but make sure you don't say the group was called something like 'The Toxic Nazis' or 'Death to Capitalism').

SKILLS

These need to be relevant to the job. The ability to ride a unicycle or juggle chainsaws, while admirable, will not really help in your job. Proficiency in languages and computer skills are useful (list all the programmes you can work in), as are things like speed reading or a photographic memory (as long as it's true!)

INTERESTS

These should show that you're sociable and also that you possess a degree of intelligence. Five-a-side football is better than solitaire, and chess is better than Twister (well, for the purposes of CVs it is, anyway). Although it's unlikely, you may be asked to demonstrate any of these skills at an interview – so make sure you're honest.

If you have published any articles, jointly or by yourself, give full details. This is of particular interest to employers since it demonstrates both writing and thinking abilities.

You never know what prejudices people have so it's best to play safe and not list anything pertaining to politics or religion.

REFERENCES

Although you don't need to list them on your CV, you should say that 'References are available on request' and have two referees 'on standby' that you've previously primed. Ideally, one of these should be work-related. Make sure the referees have a copy of your CV and don't be tempted to use relatives. You should, of course, make sure that these referees are willing to give you a reference. Give their address and both day and evening phone numbers if possible.

PERSONAL DETAILS
All you really need to give is your address, age and reiterate your phone numbers.

You don't need to list your nationality, sex or marital status, although putting 'married' and listing 'four children' hints at some sort of stability. If that gives you a warm feeling of security, put it down. (The only time you'll probably need to mention your sex is if your name does not obviously show whether you are male or female.)

TONE
Avoid the temptation to be too witty. One would-be account handler couldn't figure out why he never received interviews. His CV was good and he had worked in the marketing department at some blue-chip clients. However, under 'Interests' he had written, 'Drinking and falling over...'

Equally, avoid being too pretentious. Another unsuccessful candidate headed his CV with this quotation: 'I am imagination. I can see what the eyes cannot see. I can hear what the ears cannot hear. I can feel what the heart cannot feel.' He got filed under 'Plonker'.

THE MOST COMMON REASONS FOR CVS BEING REJECTED
From talking to agency professionals involved in recruitment, we found that these are the main reasons for CVs ending up in the bin:

● Poor visual layout
● Too long
● Misspellings, typographical errors and poor grammar
● Bad organisation of information on the page
● Not enough information about previous experience or jobs
● Insufficient reasons for the candidate to be considered at all
● Overselling the candidate

LETTERS OF APPLICATION
Alison McLeod says, 'If you're responding to a recruitment ad, highlight the relevant experience that makes you an ideal candidate for the job. If you can also get across that you know something about the company, either from the trade press or their website, then it will show you've done your homework. Keep your letter concise; the worst ones are those that ramble. And remember to include your contact details on the letter as

well as on your CV.

'If you're sending a CV on spec then point out why you are interested in that particular company. Tell them that your CV is enclosed for their consideration and that you'd be delighted to meet with them for an "open-ended discussion". Employers like this because they're not under any obligation to offer or reject you for the job – supposing that one exists anyway. It also gives them a chance to meet and get to know you without any pressure from either side'.

If you're blessed with really neat, characterful handwriting, then use this. Otherwise type it. (The MD of one large company sends handwritten letters from applicants to a graphologist to get an indication of what sort of person they are. He then decides whether it's worth interviewing them.)

Bear in mind the following:

● The letter must contain the right salutation – i.e. *Dear Mr X* or *Dear Miss Y.* Never write *Dear Sir* or *Dear Madam.* And never, ever write *Dear Sir or Madam* (you'll generally find the person you're addressing is one or the other).

● It should be as clearly and

neatly set out as your CV.

● Explain why you are writing to that particular agency, using market information gleaned from the trade press to help your application. For example, 'I read in *Campaign* that you have recently won the XYZ account and wondered if you would be staffing up in order to deal with the increased workload this international business might entail...'

● Don't be too wordy. Just say in a concise way why you would like to be considered for employment and what it is you are looking for – a job or some work experience – and in which department. Don't say that you'd appreciate 'any job'. It just shows employers that you are unfocused and/or desperate.

● Angle your letter towards the particular agency in question using information relevant to them – as if you've only sent out one CV, and it's to them. For example, tell them how you admire the work they've just done for ...... or how you were prompted to write following an article you read by their creative director in ...... magazine. Don't be too much of a brown-noser though.

● You don't know the personality of the recruiter

(unless he or she is a famous industry figure) so be careful in using humour. It *might* tickle their funny bone – or it might fall flat. You don't know so why take chances?

● Make sure you use the correct form of words when you sign off. If a letter is written to a named individual it's always 'Yours sincerely'. It's useful to remind them of your telephone number or e-mail address on your letter and never ask them to let you know if you've been successful.

FOLLOWING UP YOUR LETTER AND CV

You'll know in a week or two if you've been successful. If you haven't had an invitation for an interview or a rejection letter in this time then it's OK to write a follow-up letter to gently chase things along, acknowledging that the recruiter is probably extremely busy. You can always try calling the person or their PA but don't persevere if their line is constantly engaged. Switchboards will often give out their e-mail addresses and you're more likely to get a response by communicating this way. If you don't hear anything in a further week

then make another follow-up call or e-mail. If you don't hear anything after that, take the hint.

Take note: Rejection letters usually use the line 'we'll keep your CV on file and will notify you if future opportunities arise'. That's a lie. This file that agencies refer to is the bottom of a drawer or the bottom of the bin. You might have been unlucky in January, but that doesn't mean you shouldn't write again in July.

SOME FINAL TIPS

● If you're a student, there's probably a career advice office in your college or university. Ask them for advice.

● Use plenty of white space.

● Consider using bullet points to break up the text and make it more easily readable.

● Use the spell checker.

● Write a first draft, then go back and keep editing it until it's more concise and more readable.

● Keep copies of all letters and CVs sent, and records of telephone calls and names of the people you spoke to.

● Remember **KISS**: 'Keep It Simple, Stupid!'.

OTHER ROUTES INTO ADVERTISING

So you didn't get that place on the graduate trainee scheme at M&C Saatchi or Abbott Mead Vickers BBDO? Don't fret. Three thousand other candidates feel just as bad.

After you've come to terms with your disappointment it's time to pick yourself up, dust yourself down and begin looking at other ways to get that elusive first job.

While this section has particular relevance to account handling jobs, the advice also applies to those wishing to work in planning, media and creative services.

WORK EXPERIENCE

If you came close to a job then it might be worthwhile writing back to the agency and asking if you can have some work experience there on a temporary basis. It might not lead to anything more permanent but it will still be invaluable for your CV.

If you don't have any luck with the agency that interviewed you, write to *all* the agencies you can think of and offer your services on a temporary basis. (You won't be paid, but might get a token sum to cover travel expenses.) While success in getting a placement usually depends on being in the right place at the right time, you can help your odds by ensuring you make contact with the right person. For account handling this is usually the client services director, otherwise it's one of the board account directors responsible for media or planning (phone the switchboard and explain why you need their names, reassuring them that you are not a stalker).

In the first instance write them a letter and send a copy of your CV. Offer to work in any department if there are no opportunities in account management. It's difficult for an agency to turn someone down who's willing, able – and free. If you notice that the agency has landed a large piece of business from an existing or even a new client then write offering help on that particular account. It might be premature but at least the agency will know that you've got your eye on the ball.

If you're successful in getting temporary work it might be for a week, two weeks or a month. Be grateful for whatever period you get offered. At the same time, don't moan about the work you end up doing because in nearly all cases it will be something so menial and dull that a smarter-than-average chimp could do it.

Work experience in account-handling often involves looking up information on the Internet, checking proofs, taking stuff down to the post room or entering figures into a spreadsheet. None of this has much to do with the business of creating ads but it's the foot in the door that counts.

Use your time there to talk to as many people as you can and always go the extra mile, like working through lunch or after hours. And when you've finished a particular task, ask for another. The important thing is getting noticed and making yourself invaluable to the team you're working with.

There's a publication called the *ALF* (Account List File). Actually, its full title is 'ALF incorporating BRAD A&A', to be precise. This monthly directory lists the top 400 advertising agencies in the UK with details of their size, clients and the names of key personnel. It also cross-references the 1000 major advertisers and 9000 brands with their relevant agencies so if you're interested in working, say, on the BMW account, you can see who their agency is and

write to them (it's WCRS by the way). Oh yes, it also lists 175 industry organisations and associations.

Sounds a brilliant source doesn't it? It is. But it comes at a price. £235 for a single copy – or £795 for the year. If you're flush you could invest in a copy. If you're very flush, you could subscribe for a year. If not, ask at your local library.

The publisher is:

EMAP Media
33–39 Bowling Green Lane
LONDON EC1R 0DA
TEL 020 7505 8459
FAX 020 7505 8336

RECRUITMENT COMPANIES AND HEAD HUNTERS

Most of the jobs in advertising aren't advertised. Agencies tend to be very choosy when looking for staff so they use specialised external consultants – either recruitment agencies or head hunters – to do the work for them.

The difference between the two is simple. Candidates register with recruitment agencies and are interviewed by them. If they think you're saleable, then they'll keep your CV on their books and will send it out to ad agencies that are looking for new staff.

Head hunters work in a different way. They approach people already working in the industry to see if they're interested in moving jobs. How do they know about you? Well it's usually because your name has been mentioned to them by a colleague, a supplier, a client – or anyone that knows you and how you work. It's flattering and exciting to be called up by a head hunter. You'll recognise them because they usually give the switchboard a name that you don't recognise and the first thing they say when they phone is 'Can you talk?' (Incidentally, the fact they're called head hunters has nothing to do with them being savages. That might be a reflection on the way they poach staff but some of them are actually quite nice.)

If you're just starting out and don't have any experience, it's highly unlikely you'll be called by a head hunter, so don't sit waiting for the phone to ring.

However, it's still worth contacting recruitment companies. You can find the names of those which specialise in advertising in the back of *Campaign*, *Marketing* or *Marketing Week*. Call them first to see if you're 'saleable' and then send in your CV.

JOB RECRUITMENT ADS

While the larger agencies tend to use external consultants, many of the smaller, regional or more specialised agencies tend to advertise in the trade publications or the media sections of the national newspapers.

That means you're unlikely to see an ad that reads 'Wanted. Junior Account Executive for top London agency. Great prospects' but you might find similar jobs at a smaller business-to-business, recruitment, healthcare or niche agency anywhere in the country.

As mentioned in the **Graduate Recruitment** section, keep a look out in these publications:

● *Campaign* (out Thursday)
● *Guardian* (Media section on Monday)
● *Evening Standard* (Media section on Wednesday)
● *The Times* (Media section on Friday)
● *Independent* (Media section on Thursdays)
● *Marketing* (out Wednesday)
● *Marketing Week* (out Wednesday)

VOCATIONAL COURSES

If you read the interviews with agency staff in this book you'll notice that a lot got their foot in the door by starting in a junior position and then worked their way up. They didn't rely on qualifications to get in.

That said, with so many people applying for jobs in advertising, agencies can be very choosy about who they select for interviews, let alone who they employ. While none of the following qualifications can guarantee a job, having a vocational qualification might give you the edge over a candidate of similar standing.

These courses are worth considering:

CAM COURSES

The Communication Advertising and Marketing Education Foundation was established in 1970 to administer a range of examinations that had previously been conducted by different industry bodies. These include the Advertising Association, the Institute of Direct Marketing, the Institute of Public Relations, the Institute of Sales Promotion and the Radio Advertising Bureau – to name but a few.

The CAM qualifications have recently been revised and there are now three relating to advertising:
● The CAM Advanced Diploma in Communication Studies
● The CAM Higher Diploma in Advertising
● The CAM Higher Diploma in Integrated Marketing Communications – available from September 2000. (If that qualification doesn't sound impressive then what does?)

Courses can be taken through full-time study, evening classes or intensive weekend classes at a number of colleges around the country. Alternatively there are distance-learning programmes available. Contact the CAM Foundation for more information and a syllabus.

● THE CAM ADVANCED DIPLOMA IN COMMUNICATION STUDIES

Entry requirements:

Candidates must be over 18, preferably with a degree but as a minimum, five GCSE passes grade C and above including English and Maths (or the equivalent qualifications).

The course:

Candidates take and have to pass six modules to demonstrate a broad understanding of these areas: marketing; advertising; PR; media; direct mail and sales promotion; research and consumer behaviour.

● THE CAM HIGHER DIPLOMA IN ADVERTISING

Entry requirements:
Successful completion of the Advanced Diploma (above). In some cases experienced practitioners can still sit this if they can prove their experience and competence and have a relevant educational background.

The course:
Candidates take three modules: Management and Strategy; Consumer Advertising; Business-to-Business Advertising. (This course is positioned as a postgraduate qualification.)

● THE CAM HIGHER DIPLOMA IN INTEGRATED MARKETING COMMUNICATIONS

Entry requirements:
Successful completion of the Higher Diploma in Advertising (above) *plus* the Higher Diploma in Public Relations (also run by the CAM Foundation).

The course:
Candidates take a paper in Planning, Implementation and Evaluation. This, and the knowledge they've gained in advertising and PR will show a candidate how to successfully manage an integrated communications campaign.

Further details from:

The CAM Foundation
Abford House
15 Wilton Road
LONDON SW1V 1NJ
TEL 020 7828 7506
FAX 020 7976 5140
E-MAIL
info@camfoundation.com
WEBSITE
www.camfoundation.com

● THE WEST HERTS COLLEGE POSTGRADUATE DIPLOMA IN ADVERTISING

Running since 1971, this 30-week course covers a multitude of subjects including: advertising; campaign planning; media; marketing; market research; copywriting; art direction; consumer behaviour; advertising law; sales pro-motion; presentation skills; direct response; desktop publishing; plus a choice of workshops in either radio or video.

It's the only course in the UK that's accredited by the

International Advertising Association, which means that it has international recognition (and therefore, should impress the personnel manager at Young and Rubicam in Caracas).

Former students speak very highly of this course which is very practical, giving candidates first-hand experience working on briefs set by real agencies, planning campaigns and creating work to present to real clients. The course also attracts visiting speakers from the leading ad agencies and includes a visit to a top London agency.

Entry requirements:
Candidates must hold a degree, an IAA Diploma, a BTEC High Diploma or other recognised degree-level qualification. Mature students are also considered if they can prove extensive work experience in advertising or a related field.

The course is usually over subscribed and to be considered for it, as well as sending a written application, students also have to create an advertisement selling themselves and enclose an existing advertisement they think is ineffective, saying how it could be improved.

Further details from:
The Course Director
Postgraduate Diploma in Advertising
Watford School of Business
West Herts College
Hampstead Road
WATFORD
Herts WD1 3EZ
TEL 01923 812591
FAX 01923 812584
E-MAIL andrean@westherts.ac.uk
WEBSITE www.westherts.ac.uk

There are far too many courses to be listed here in detail and syllabi can and do change. However here are some other useful contact details:

● **THE CHARTERED INSTITUTE OF MARKETING (CIM)**
Moor Hall
Cookham
MAIDENHEAD
Berkshire SL6 9QH
TEL 01628 427500
WEBSITE www.cim.co.uk

As you'd expect, the CIM offers professional qualifications (CIM certificate and CIM Diploma) in marketing as well as a wide range of short courses in subjects including brand marketing, service marketing, international marketing and e-commerce.

● **THE INSTITUTE OF DIRECT MARKETING (IDM)**
1 Park Road
Teddington
Middlesex
TW11 0AR
TEL 020 8977 5705
WEBSITE www.theidm.co.uk

The IDM offers a Certificate and a Diploma in Direct Marketing.

The certificate is taught in eight modules over two intensive three-day sessions which include examinations. The diploma can be taken via a number of options including evening classes, residential and non-residential courses and via distance learning. A postgraduate MA in Direct Marketing is also offered as a part-time block release course.

Short-term courses in these subjects are also offered: relationship marketing, business-to-business, database marketing, new media and technology and telebusiness.

● **THE INSTITUTE OF SALES PROMOTION (ISP)**
Arena House
66-68 Pentonville Road
Islington
London N1 9HS
TEL 020 7837 5340
WEBSITE www.isp.org.uk

The ISP Diploma is a recognised practical qualification for those wishing to work in the area of sales promotion. It's a four-month distance-learning programme supported by a series of evening tutorials throughout the course.

Other courses run by the ISP include a one-day basics course designed specifically for people new to sales promotion and a three-day foundation course designed to give candidates a very broad understanding of the key issues relevant to running successful promotions.

● **BA (HONS) ADVERTISING AND MARKETING**
● **BA (HONS) ADVERTISING AND MARKETING COMMUNICATIONS**

Universities and Colleges offering these degrees include:
● **West Herts College**
TEL 01923 812591
WEBSITE www.westherts.ac.uk
● **Bournemouth University**
TEL 01202 524111
WEBSITE www.bournemouth.ac.uk
● **Lancaster University**
TEL 01524 65201
WEBSITE www.lancaster.ac.uk
● **University of Luton**
TEL 01582 734111
WEBSITE www.luton.ac.uk

There are many other degrees in marketing and communications. For the latest information, refer to the University and College Admissions Service (UCAS) website at: **www.ucas.ac.uk**. The IPA website also has information on relevant courses under its 'careers' section: **www.ipa.co.uk**.

LONDON COLLEGE OF PRINTING SHORT-TERM COURSES

The London College of Printing is a misnomer. Yes it does offer some very good courses in printing technology and management, but it also offers a very wide range of useful short courses in all manner of other advertising-related subjects including desktop publishing, retouching, website design and radio production. These are of particular relevance as a general introduction to the industry:

● Advertising (2 days or 6 evenings)
● Advertising, PR and Promotion (2 weeks)
● Direct Marketing (1 day)
● Introduction to Marketing and Sales Promotion (2 days or 6 evenings)
● Publicity and Promotion (1 day)

● Marketing and Advertising (10 weeks)
● Marketing on the Internet (2 days)

Full details of each of these courses (which take place at the Elephant and Castle, London SE1), including dates and fees, can be obtained from:

The London College of Printing
Elephant & Castle
LONDON SE1 6SB
TEL 020 7514 6770
WEBSITE www.lcp.linst.ac.uk

Other, more specific courses at the LCP are listed at the end of the relevant job sections.

NETWORKING

A lot of successful people in advertising got their first break because they knew someone. It might have been their next-door neighbour, that dodgy old bloke who works in the post room, or it might have been their cousin's girlfriend's step-dad's best mate who sold the agency its photocopiers and knows the office manager.

It doesn't matter who it is. Just remember that there's no shame in getting started this way. Hundreds of people have done it and if you don't take advantage of as many contacts as you can – irrespective of how tenuous they are – then someone else will.

Send a letter to everyone you can think of, telling them about your plight and asking for any contact they can think of. Ask them to put it on their office notice boards or send an inter-office e-mail to spread the net wider.

Another way of networking is to hang out at pubs near agencies so you get a chance to mix with, and hopefully meet, agency staff. A wannabe account handler frequented the Barley Mow pub just off Baker Street, which was usually packed at the time with staff from three large agencies, DDB, Euro, and FCB. He printed up copies of his CV and with the permission of the landlord, handed these out. It didn't take long before he was offered a job as a production assistant. Not the job he wanted but that all-important first step.

CREATE YOUR OWN WEBSITE

Most Internet Servive Providers (ISPs) these days offer free web space and advice on how to create your own site and upload it. One way of getting noticed is to create your own site, which is, in effect, your CV. It needn't be complicated – just a couple of pages including a photograph of yourself will do.

You can then send a note to, or e-mail, prospective employers advising them about your site. If nothing else, it shows how keen you are to get a job, how inventive you are, plus alerts them to the fact that you've created the site yourself. How's that for initiative? (Just don't fill your site with dancing hamsters or hyperlinks to dodgy triple-x sites!)

HOW TO GET INTO THE CREATIVE DEPARTMENT

● **WARNING:** If you want to work in Account Handling, Media or Planning, don't read this section. Go to **Graduate Training Schemes** instead.

In this section we're looking at how would-be art directors or copywriters get a job at an agency. If you're reading this book and aren't sure what these people do, then read the relevant sections for both job functions, then come back here. We'll wait.

For the rest of you who have already decided that working in one of these roles is just what you want to do, good luck (you'll need it)!

Getting a job in the creative department is difficult, there's no hiding that fact. As with account handlers who want to get on graduate trainee schemes, the positions are so oversubscribed that agencies can be very picky about who they want working for them. And since an agency's product is its ideas, then it has to make damn sure that the people on its payroll in the creative department are able to come up with the most original and best executed ideas, day after day.

But don't let that put you off, or make you feel too pressurised.

These are interesting times for art directors and copywriters as there's a trend towards change in the way they work. In the late 50s/early 60s, when the concept of the modern full-service agency became popular, art directors and copywriters usually led quite separate lives. The art director would decide on the look of the ad or commercial and then hand this over to the copywriter who would write text or dialogue. In many cases they worked in separate offices.

Throughout the 70s and 80s the roles remained pretty much the same but the concept of a creative 'team' evolved – pairs of art directors and copywriters almost joined at the hip, sharing an office. They worked together like Morecambe and Wise or Cannon and Ball. Well, preferably more like Morecambe and Wise.

Nowadays, however, the distinction between copywriters and art directors is more blurred and in larger agencies, both have an equal input on the words and the pictures.

This trend began in the United States and one of the pioneers was Chiat Day which encouraged teams, led by planners, to explore ideas – rather than just dumping the brief in the creative department, walking away and looking at the work a week later. It's a way of working that recognises that good ideas on copy and the way an ad looks can come from anyone – if they're creative enough.

Vicki MaGuire, a copywriter at Ogilvys says, 'The industry and the way we work are changing. A lot of agencies still work in conventional teams but there's more of a move towards brainstorming. Ideas are important and five people in a room bouncing ideas off each other can be much more effective'.

Don Beardsworth, an art director at St Luke's says, 'Thirty years ago an art director would never touch copy and a copywriter would never dream of, say, commenting on a font. It was just unheard of.'

By now you may be concerned that you can think visually but not write copy. Or vice versa. Don't worry. Not that many people are talented at both and in the majority of agencies, art directors and copywriters are still separate breeds, and in no danger of extinction.

Most agencies only hire creative teams, not creative individuals, which means the first thing you need to do is find a partner. But as well as a partner you'll also need a portfolio of your work. This serves two purposes. The first is to get you a partner. The second is to get both of you a job. This portfolio is called the Book.

It's got a capital 'B' because it's that important. Your Book will be a representation of your work and you'll be hired on the quality of this. It doesn't matter if you're as suave as Clark Gable, as good looking as Cary Grant or as dynamic and thrusting as Errol Flynn (if you're a bloke, that is) – if your Book isn't up to scratch, you won't get that job.

HOW TO GET A BOOK TOGETHER

It's all well and good telling you to get a portfolio of your work together, but how do you go about it? There are three main ways to compile your Book. It might well be a combination of all three methods. (If you're at college you should still consider supplementing the work you've done by making up your own briefs – see method 2. This will greatly add to the variety of your work.)

1 If you're at college then the work in your Book could be course or project work.

2 If you're not formally studying advertising, copywriting or design, but feel that you're creative, then you can invent your own creative briefs – and work up ads that answer them. For example, 'promote a watch that's solar powered, so you never have to buy a battery again', 'promote a new fizzy drink that smells as well as tastes of lemons', 'promote a new chain of hamburger restaurants where you only pay what you think the meal is worth'. The briefs you set yourself are only limited by your imagination – and if you're no good at that, well, maybe you should think again about a creative career!

3 You can include creative work from D&AD Advertising Workshops (see notes below).

IMPORTANT

However you compile your Book, remember that it should never, ever stay static. Always keep it updated with examples of newer and better work. If you're fortunate enough to get a work placement, then include

work from here. Even during your professional career you'll be constantly updating your book to take with you to interviews.

FORMAT

Books usually follow the same format – a carrying case with an integral ring binder that holds A3 sheets in clear plastic sleeves. These are available from all art supply shops.

The ads in your Book can be in black and white or colour (most tend to be in black and white) and are usually hand drawn using a thick felt pen.

The people who'll be looking at your work won't be bothered about how good the drawings are. They're concerned about the ideas behind your ads. You should spend far more time working on the concepts than on actually executing them. (But that's not to say that the book can be scrappy. It needs to have a fair degree of finish if you want to be taken seriously.)

CONTENT

Basically, your best work. Remember, your Book will be used to attract the other half of your creative team as well as trying to get you hired. Once your creative partner is on board then you'll work together on improving the Book, starting with including the best of your own, individual work. You could suggest a better way of executing one of your partner's ideas. Equally, they might suggest a better headline for one of yours. Don't be precious. If you are, then the team is doomed to an early divorce. Remember that you want to present the best work possible. Don't let individual pride or dignity get in the way of this.

VARIETY

Agencies want to see creativity across a number of media so include ads designed to appear in the national press and magazines, on TV, posters and maybe even the web. Apart from looking for creativity in the messages, agencies are also looking for innovative uses of those media. Don't think you have to think 'big'. Some really strong ideas can be executed in small spaces.

Take a leaf out of TV producers' books. They'll put the best shows in a series at the beginning and end and 'hide' mediocre ones in the middle.

Ideally your book should have good work all the way through and there shouldn't be anything mediocre at all. If this is the case (we hope it is), then put the extraordinarily great work at the beginning and end and just the great work in the middle.

Finally, make sure you've got a good cross-section of work. Don't fill your Book with ten campaigns for tampons, or ten campaigns aimed at single young men.

Show diversity across products and target audience. (**Tip:** Avoid including too many ads for charities. That and sex aids. Everyone does them.)

BE FOCUSED

Decide which sort of agency you want to work for and target your Book to suit their requirements. If you want to work for a recruitment agency, then there's no point taking along a Book of TV and poster executions. Suppose though, that you wanted to work in a specialist area such as business-to-business or healthcare, then your Book should show a lot of trade magazine ads. And if you did want to work in an agency that handles a lot of TV work then your Book should have a bias towards storyboards.

QUANTITY

It's quality not quantity that counts here. Agencies are not impressed by volume so don't get tempted to include twenty different campaigns – most agencies suggest that between eight and ten or twelve is enough. The key word here is campaigns. A campaign is a series of different executions which all meet the brief but in different ways. This is to keep the audience entertained and prevent them getting bored too easily. A campaign can also be a progression of executions over a period of time that tell a story, as in the case of Nescafe's Gold Blend commercials.

Either way, agencies want to see how you can develop your thinking across an advertising proposition. That's why it's better to have eight different campaigns rather than twelve different one-off ads.

ADVICE ON JOINING THE CREATIVE DEPARTMENT

● Don't think you know it all just because you did well in college.
● Don't do it for the money, there isn't as much as you think. It's no longer the 80s.
● Be prepared to change your Book drastically and that could involve changing everything.
● Don't overfinish work. It's the idea that counts, not the art direction or access to a Mac.
● If you want to do TV keep it

simple, as few frames as possible with a minimum of written explanation. Otherwise people just won't read it. If you have to explain an idea, it doesn't work.
● Visit lots of teams and agencies. Get to know as many people as possible.
● Remember it's only one team's opinion, not the agency's – or the industry's for that matter.
● Be prepared to work hard on your Book for anything from a year to three or four years. So if you're not 100% committed... don't bother!
● Never burn your bridges. You never know where someone might turn up.
● Be willing to learn!
● Have fun. And remember some people have to work for a living.

Source: British Design and Art Direction, 2000

HOW DO I FIND A PARTNER?

Like the best marriages, you and your partner must complement each other. Yes, you'll each have strengths and weaknesses and you need to recognise this. It won't take long after meeting up to know whether you and your creative partner click and there's a long term future in it.

A) AT COLLEGE/ UNIVERSITY

There might be someone on your design or marketing course who complements your style. If not, advertise in the college magazine or on its notice board. It's also worth mentioning to your lecturers that you're looking for a partner. They might know of someone, or could discuss it with other members of the faculty.

B) AT AN END OF DEGREE SHOW

After a design or advertising-related course there's usually an end of degree show where students display samples of their work and contact details. Advertising agencies come to this show looking for new talent – though it's rare that anyone is actually hired here. They're of more use as an opportunity to meet your creative partner.

C) APPROACH CREATIVE RECRUITMENT COMPANIES

You'll see these companies advertising at the back of *Campaign* magazine. It doesn't do any harm to ask them if they've been approached by anyone at your level also looking for a partner.

D) AT AN AGENCY

Although most agencies recruit teams, if your Book is good enough they might consider pairing you with an existing creative, whose previous partner might have left. (It's far easier to find employment as half of a conventional team though.)

E) VIA D&AD

On the entry form to their advertising workshops (see below), candidates are asked if they are working alone, and if so do they want their name and telephone number passed to other creatives looking to team up.

GETTING YOUR BOOK SEEN

So you've got your partner and your Book. Well done (that was the easy part). Now's the time for you to hawk it round the agencies like a door-to-door encyclopaedia salesman.

The first thing to do is call the creative secretary or the creative director's PA and ask if there's a chance that someone could see your Book. Opportunities are limited and there's usually a quota per week or per month. It's rare for you to be there while someone's looking at your work. Normally you'll get a call telling you that it's ready for collection. If you're lucky you'll get feedback, either in a note or over the phone. Sometimes though, you'll just get your Book back, and you won't have a clue whether it was good, bad or just plain ugly. The chances are though, that if it didn't get a response, it's probably because whoever saw the Book didn't rate it. This is far from satisfactory, since what you're looking for are useful comments, but be prepared for it.

Don Beardsworth, an art director at St. Luke's, says, 'I trained to be an art director and met my copywriter at my end of year show at St Martin's School of Art. He came to the show, saw my work and liked it and got in touch. We got our portfolio together, working up all our favourite ideas. We then went on a tour of the agencies. You phone up, make an appointment (which is usually cancelled) and show your Book to one of the creative teams there who'll hopefully give you some constructive criticism. You usually find that you'll get a completely different view from each team you see!'

In some cases you're there while your work is being critiqued and this gives you the chance to discuss the thought process you went through in coming up with the idea. This might be the first time you're in the hallowed presence of a Real Creative Team. Be calm. Breathe deeply. And don't let what they say put you off. You may politely disagree if they savagely criticise one of your campaigns – but at your peril and only if you think they've misinterpreted something. Don't lose your rag and storm out clutching your precious work. You'll be the butt of jokes in Charlotte Street pubs and bars for days to come and word will get around to other agencies that you're a pair of idiots.

One half of a creative team was petrified when he discovered that his Book was being critiqued by one of the highest profile creative directors of the time, a particularly highly-strung gentleman. He had taken it upon himself to look for new talent and flicked through their Book very slowly, taking in everything and not saying a single word. Eventually he closed the book, handed it to the would-be copywriter and said very haughtily. 'Frankly, if I were you, I wouldn't bother'.

His attitude is a terrible advertisement for the industry and it so undermined the confidence of the copywriter that he left the industry completely and set up a business selling fresh fish.

It does show, however, that you need to be thick-skinned and resilient. One creative director describes the best art directors and copywriters as Weebles; they wobble but they don't fall down.

If you do get helpful comments on any of your work from an agency then take these on board. They usually know what they're talking about. It might also give you the chance to get back in and show them your improvements – along with some other work you want them to see.

WORK PLACEMENT
The aim of showing your Book to the advertising Great and Good is to land yourself a placement. If you're fortunate, you'll find yourself with one or two weeks' work and get paid between nothing and a token sum of about £50 per week to cover travel.

The real benefit is that you've got a foot in the door. You're in a real working environment and you're working on a real brief, albeit not a high-profile one. But be prepared to be treated as work placement creatives. Don't be surprised to find the two of you sharing a windowless office designed for one person, working on promoting ball bearings or incontinence trousers. Don't worry, it's a start.

You'll often find that agencies see a number of teams on placement, one after the other, who are all competing for the same job. In a few cases you might be lucky enough to get a job offer immediately after your stint. In most cases, though, if you're selected, you'll get invited back after the agency has seen their quota of teams.

If so, congratulations. You've landed that difficult 'first job'!

CREATIVE MAILINGS
If you can't get past the creative secretary to get your Book seen, then there are other ways. One tried and tested route is to send in a creative CV. Creatives are expected to be, well, creative. That's why it's OK for them to send in unusual, inventive or just plain wacky CVs to grab someone's attention.

(**Take note:** This advice doesn't apply to would-be account handlers, media buyers or planners who have their own section, **CV Tips** (p.29), which is dull but more applicable to 'suits'.)

One ruse included a team sending the creative director a packet of peanuts a day for a month. He couldn't figure out what on earth was happening until the last bag was accompanied by a letter asking for a job, saying that they'd work for... you've guessed it... peanuts. They got a placement.

One team sent the head of copy and the head of art each a pair of sunglasses because they were 'this year's brightest graduates'. They got an interview.

A would-be art director approached BBDO by sending them a letter together with a cut-out tracing of his foot. His letter began, 'Now that I've got a foot in the door...' He too got his interview. You can probably do better. If you can't, you're probably considering the wrong career.

BRITISH DESIGN AND ART DIRECTION (D&AD)

The highest accolade a creative can get is being awarded a D&AD Gold or Silver Pencil at their annual awards ceremony. Last year over 17,000 different submissions were entered across 20 categories and 91 entries were shortlisted for 39 awards.

But apart from recognising the highest standards of creativity, D&AD also places a high priority on education and offers a range of programmes and student competitions that seek to identify new creative talents and develop and train them.

These are open to young creative teams who are not in full-time employment in the advertising and design industries.

ADVERTISING WORKSHOPS

Creative workshops for aspiring young art directors and copywriters have been held by the D&AD for more than ten years and are a well-recognised route to a job. Many of the creative teams that host the workshops were actually once delegates themselves. According to D&AD, 'The workshops provide a unique opportunity for aspiring art directors or copywriters to work on advertising briefs and have their work reviewed and appraised by creative teams from top advertising agencies.'

These workshops are held in London, Edinburgh, Leeds and Manchester. However, entry is limited to 22 people who are pre-selected on their ability by working on an initial creative brief. (There is a small registration fee to get on the course.)

The successful applicants are invited to attend the workshops which take place over six weeks. Each week, creatives from a different agency set a brief and then critique the work a week later. At the end of this session you receive the brief for the next week – and so on. When the course is completed all participants receive a certificate and a 'best Book of the course' prize is awarded. This is usually a placement in a top London agency.

These workshops are open to anyone with a creative flair, not just students studying a creative discipline. Previous courses have included accountants, secretaries, plumbers – even account handlers.

COMPETITIONS:

STUDENT AWARDS

Students are invited to submit work based on real clients' briefs across 23 design and advertising disciplines. All the winners have their work published in the glossy D&AD Student Awards Annual which is seen by 1700 potential employers. Having work published in the annual is a real coup and stands creative teams in very good stead for obtaining work placements.

D&AD CANNES YOUNG CREATIVE COMPETITION

Anyone can submit five pieces of work from their portfolio. From these, judges will shortlist a number of teams who are then invited to present their whole portfolio at a final judging session. The winners receive an all-expenses paid trip to Cannes, £500 prize money, plus, of course, a good chance of landing a job when they get back.

Take note: D&AD have requested that this book makes it clear that they do NOT, repeat NOT, organise placements for students.

For further information and entry or application forms contact British Design & Art Direction (address overleaf).

PS Did we make it clear that D&AD do *not* organise placements for students?

USEFUL ADDRESSES
British Design & Art Direction
9 Graphite Square
Vauxhall Walk
LONDON SE11 5EE
TEL 020 7840 1111
FAX 020 7840 0840
WEBSITE www.dandad.org

Campaign Magazine
174 Hammersmith Road
LONDON W6 7JP
TEL 020 7413 4570
WEBSITE
www.campaignlive.com

The Advertising Association
Abford House
15 Wilton Road
LONDON SW1 1NJ
TEL 020 7828 2771
WEBSITE www.adassoc.org.uk
The Advertising Association
has a library with information
on ad agencies, but all visits
are by appointment only.

ACCOUNT MANAGEMENT

MONEY: What a minefield! Salaries vary according to the size and structure of the agency, your experience and the type of the clients you are handling. That's why an account executive in a large agency might earn more than an account manager somewhere else.

● Account Executives: £15,000 – £24,000; Account Managers/Supervisors: £25,000 – £32,000; Account Directors: £32,000 – £45,000+ (Nearly all account director positions include a company car. Some account managers' jobs too).

HOURS: At least 8; normally 10-12 but again, usually dependent on the agency structure and type of client. Handling international clients requires you not only to put in the hours at the UK office, but to make/take calls at your client's local time (which isn't much fun if you're working on the Brisbane Tourist Board account).

● Leisure plays only a small part of your weekend. The rest of the time tends to be taken up with writing strategies and reading sales reports.

HEALTH RISK: 2/10. Account handlers are never employed for their heavy-lifting or paragliding abilities, therefore over-indulgence while entertaining clients is the only real inherent danger.

Stress, however, is another matter (see below).

Would-be account handlers should take comfort in the fact that the job is far safer now than it was in the 1980s when being punched, or having a chair thrown at you by an irate creative because his work wasn't accepted was an occupational hazard.

PRESSURE RATING: 8/10. If your client has been with the agency for 15 years and accounts for 40% of its profits then you'll find that prolific sweating and ulcers are as natural to you as breathing.

GLAMOUR RATING: 3/10 to 10/10. There's not much glamour in flying up to East Kilbride on a wet Tuesday morning to present the latest trade press ad for a new, improved brand of oven cleaner. However, the opposite is true when you're in New Mexico for a week, making sure that the TV commercial for the launch of a new sports coupé is going exactly as planned. It all depends on the products you're promoting.

● Remember, for every up-market drinks company that needs an agency to promote its wares, there are ten companies selling things like industrial sumps and drainage equipment, plasterboard and rat poisons.

TRAVEL RATING: 3/10 to 10/10. See above.

NOTE:

Let's get things straight. Advertising agencies have clients, which are known as 'accounts'. This has nothing to do with the accounts department and confuses the hell out of anyone who works outside the industry:

'What do you do?'

I work for an ad agency. I'm an account manager.'

'Really. I didn't know you were an accountant.'

I'm not. I'm an account manager. I look after some of our agency's accounts.'

'What? You do their book keeping?'

No. Our accounts are our clients.'

'So you do book keeping for your clients?'

No! Listen!!! In advertising we call our clients our accounts.'

'Are you a chartered accountant then?'

What's also confusing is trying to define individual roles at each level of account management. It all depends on the nature of the agency and its management structure. Some agencies distinguish between junior account executives and account executives. A few have the role of account supervisor but in some it's used instead of account manager, while in others it's a position between account executive and account manager. And don't even ask about senior account directors.

As life is complicated enough we've decided to group all these various roles into this larger section called 'Account Management'. For ease of description, we'll call all these people 'account handlers'.

No matter how high up the account management ladder you are (or even if you're at the bottom holding it for someone so it doesn't wobble), the job is basically the same.

You're there as the pivotal interface between the agency (and in particular, the creative department) and the client, getting grief more than you get praise.

It's a dirty job but someone's got to do it.

The account executives, supervisors, managers and directors are the front men (and women); the public face of the agency and the clients' regular contacts. As such, they have to please both their agency and their clients despite torn loyalties.

Agencies want to produce highly creative work which meets business objectives and gains kudos and awards. Most clients are happy with campaigns that just meet their business objectives – even if this means they're not the most creative.

You know the expression 'between a rock and a hard place'? Well, that's where the account handler lives.

If you've got the tact of Prince Philip, the personality of Charles Manson and the creative appreciation of a BBC commissioning editor then you should really think again about being an account handler. Maybe you should become a client instead.

Account handlers are key players in the agency. Good ones will build up a rapport with their clients and develop a long-term, mutually beneficial relationship. Bad ones will alienate clients, lose the agency their business and ultimately lose themselves their job.

Most account handlers work in structured teams and handle a number of different accounts at any one time. The team hierarchy normally corresponds with that of the client's own marketing or advertising team.

So what do account handlers actually do? Well, at the risk of shattering the illusions of those who remember *Thirtysomething,* they do not spend a large part of their day shooting baskets and shooting the bull with colleagues (although the recurring sub-plot about being intimidated by the creative director does have a certain ring of truth about it).

In simple terms, clients have various marketing requirements that require advertising solutions. For example, the company might need to increase consumer awareness of its green policies, influence shareholders about a take-over bid, reveal a new corporate identity, announce 20p off a new ice cream, launch a brand new product or even relaunch a tired old one.

Clients want their agency to deliver the most suitable solutions, on time and within budget and it is the account handler's job (led by the account director) to achieve this. As the account team looking after a particular client, you're also acting as the client's 'brand guardian'. This means that you have to ensure that the values inherent in a certain company or its brands are retained and certainly never undermined by anything the agency does.

It's the account director's role (and planner's, if the agency has this discipline) to steer the creative work in the right direction to meet the client's objectives, and the account manager's role, assisted by the account executive, to ensure it's implemented and executed correctly. OK, these are simple divisions. In reality it's a team effort with these sorts of responsibilities:

ACCOUNT EXECUTIVES

They tend to be responsible for the day-to-day running and administration of an account. They're the people in the meetings taking minutes for the **contact reports,** making sure that all paperwork and filing is done. They make sure the **brand book** is always updated, they prepare estimates and timing plans, gather research material, chase agency departments like production and traffic, and sometimes suppliers, and generally assist the account manager. The smooth running of the account team normally relies on their tea- and coffee-making proficiency.

ACCOUNT MANAGERS/ ACCOUNT SUPERVISORS

As the 'middle rank' between account executive and account director, there's more of a blurring of roles here, particularly when some account groups won't have an account executive – just a manager and a director. The account manager/supervisor basically oversees everything the account executive is doing and would probably draft the creative or copy briefs, working in conjunction with the account director, and also brief the creative teams. They might also take responsibility for **billing** the client each month.

ACCOUNT DIRECTORS

Broadly speaking, account directors are responsible, sometimes with a planner, for developing the strategy and the creative work in order to meet the client's business objectives on both product and corporate level.

The account director should have an overview of what's happening on any project but won't get involved in the nitty-gritty day-to-day detail. It's not a question of being lazy – or even not having enough time. It's about having faith in your team. Successful account directors run their team as a tight ship and are aware of everything that's going on, even though they're at arm's length from it.

As head of this team, the account director has to ensure that every member of it provides the right level of service. Although creativity is subjective, service is easily quantifiable. It's difficult to assess whether an ad is 'good', 'great' or even 'brilliant', but a client will always remember if his urgent call took three hours to be returned, or if the contact report from the meeting took three days to arrive. It's important that the level of commitment to the client is echoed all the way down. You want the relationship with the client to be good at all levels – not just yours.

Nicki Hill is an account executive at AMD (Advertising Marketing and Design). She's been in this role for about nine months and her account team consists of her, a board director and an account director. Because of this structure she has a lot of autonomy in her role.

She says, 'I was hired as a graduate trainee and I thought I was going to work in the PR department. I actually knew very little about PR and very little about advertising, having done my degree in French and English. My interviewer obviously thought that my strengths would lie in advertising instead of PR (luckily) and here I am – landing in it completely by default.

'My job entails day-to-day administration like client and supplier correspondence, the preparation of estimates, taking minutes in client meetings and issuing contact reports. A vital role is making sure that the right ads get sent out to the right papers and magazines to meet deadlines. I get involved in creative meetings with the client and also internal discussions. One of my biggest tasks was dealing with the agents of three well-known Olympic athletes who were endorsing one of my client's products in a press campaign. I had to chase the contracts, make sure both sides were happy with them and make sure they were signed. I also liaised with the photographer who was shooting the athletes and made sure that everything and everyone was in the right place at the right time.

"There's no typical day! As you set out your agenda one evening for the next day you think, perfect, I know exactly what I can accomplish tomorrow and I will have time to deal with it all. Before 9 a.m. has rolled around the next day you have already been putting out fires. Having said this, it's what keeps the job interesting and exciting and I much prefer it like this than something boring and predictable.

'In this role you have to be creative and have good people skills. You've got to demonstrate a willingness to work hard and work under pressure because of the tight deadlines we work to. You've got to be organised, be able to think fast and think laterally. It's a stressful job and the worst thing you can do is be impatient.

'The best thing I like about my job, apart from the great people I work with, is the chance to produce some fantastic creative work and having the opportunity to conceive new and different creative ideas and see them come to fruition.

'The worst part is having to answer to clients' whims on a continual basis and sometimes compromising what you think is the best possible work the creative team is producing because a client doesn't like it.'

QUALIFICATIONS

As far as qualifications for account handlers go, there's no hard-and-fast rule and there are as many graduates as non-graduates in the role. One of the authors of this book, now an agency director, started off as a studio junior (although some say he should have stayed there).

However, whatever your formal qualifications, it's a job that requires a modicum of intelligence. On one hand you need to have an ability to assimilate a lot of market information. Depending on the type of business you are working on and its sophistication, you might need to be able to interpret data like sales reports, market intelligence and research results and provide a strategy or brief based on this information. On the other hand, you need to have an appreciation of the creative product and be able to articulate your views.

Nicki Hill says, 'Although I've got a degree I think the right traits are more important than qualifications. These include patience (when dealing with a client on one side and a creative person on the other); diplomatic skills for dealing with the client; a sense of excitement for the product you're marketing and the ability to remain organised and calm all of the time. I don't think that someone needs to have a degree in an advertising or marketing related subject to do well in this field. There are plenty of people who have general degrees who qualify, and might even be better suited as they come from a better-rounded educational base.'

Publicity Overload is a small full-service agency. Established over twenty years ago and predominantly specialising in business-to-business accounts, it has taken on a number of first timers as trainee account executives over the years. What do they look for in an applicant?

'We rarely – if ever – get applications from someone with an advertising or advertising-related degree,' says managing director John Choopani. 'That's fine. If someone has a degree *per se*, it's proof that they're bright and able. We can take that ability and bring them on. They learn on the job.

'What I'm ideally looking for are people with some creativity about them. They're very rare, I promise you. At an interview, I'm also looking for enthusiasm and a lively sense of humour. I ask myself if my clients would like this person and – frankly – am I enjoying this interview? I'm also keen to make sure that they're prepared to muck in. In a small agency, there are lots of different jobs to be done. Some are quite menial. If an applicant thinks they're above franking the post or stuffing some envelopes when necessary then we don't want them...'

WHERE DO APPLICANTS GO WRONG?

'When they go to extremes,' says John, 'applicants who are very sheepish make interviews a pain. They sit there all quiet and withdrawn and you have to coax each answer out of them. Equally, applicants who are too lively at interview often come over as flippant. You don't get the impression that they care about getting the job – or that they'll stay very long. I want people who take an interview seriously – because they're more likely to take the job seriously. You'd also be surprised just how many applicants make a good impression at a first interview and then blow it at the second. Maybe they're more nervous, I don't know. Sometimes they're like chalk and cheese...'

(See the separate section on **Graduate Training Schemes**.)

ACCOUNT HANDLERS AND THEIR ROLE WITHIN THE AGENCY

In the process of creating advertising to meet the particular objectives set by the client, account handlers will liaise with various agency departments. However, the task starts with compiling as much information as possible (from the client and other sources) relating to the product, the target audience, buying patterns, competitive activity, other influences on purchase – and anything else that's relevant.

The account director and planner will work together to devise a strategy that will (hopefully) meet the client's objectives. This strategy will include a media brief and a creative brief. In agencies without a planning function, the account team can work on this together, sometimes with the help of creatives.

In simple terms, the media brief will identify the target audience (who the advertising is aimed at), the period of advertising and the budget. This leads to a media schedule being devised showing when and where the ads would run, be it via TV, national press, women's magazines radio, posters, the Internet, etc.

Similarly, the creative brief will identify the main point to be communicated in the advertisement, supporting information that has to be conveyed, whether a single ad or campaign is needed and, importantly, the 'tone of voice' – for example, authoritative, friendly, young, humorous, professional, etc. The creative department will work from this brief in developing their ideas.

All through this process, the account director will use their knowledge of the client and his business to help steer the creative work in the right direction. He'll host internal meetings and reviews to help refine the work until it's deemed suitable to present. Hours can be spent arguing over different creative approaches. Or even the brief itself. Is it correct? Is advertising really the most effective way of communicating the message? Would PR or direct mail be more effective?

To be an effective account handler, at whatever level, you'll need to have the courage of your convictions, as well as an open mind. In some cases the brief might have to be re-assessed and you should be willing to accept this. At the end of the day there should be no problem in going back to the client and saying that – after careful consideration – they shouldn't spend money on a TV commercial since an in-store promotion would be more cost-effective. At least it shows the agency has a degree of integrity and has really thought around the problem. (However, don't bring this up two weeks before the commercial is due to be screened and after £250,000 has already been spent on it.)

At any one time, you might be working on a number of projects, all with different objectives over different time spans. To some, it's this variation that makes the job so attractive.

'I work on a chain of electrical appliance stores', says Keith Davey, an account director at a large regional advertising agency. 'This is a highly competitive market and we're always working on a number of marketing initiatives in order to maintain and grow our client's market share. A marketing programme is worked out well in advance so we know what's being promoted throughout the year, be it camcorders, hi-fi systems, cookers, fridges, games consoles, computers etc., At the

moment I'm working on a new TV commercial and poster campaign in support of their sale and a mailer to send to all customers on their database. We're also looking at the branding for new in-store displays and commissioning research into customer awareness and satisfaction'.

Paul Graham is an account supervisor at M&C Saatchi who has been at the agency for three years since graduating. He says, 'My role entails ensuring the smooth running of my accounts – i.e. keeping the client happy, driving the strategic and creative processes within the agency and ensuring good relationships with all involved. To do this sort of job effectively you've got to have an outgoing personality, be adaptable and be able to learn quickly. You've also got to be trustworthy, have good attention to detail (or a dedication to learn how!), and an eye for creativity.

'What I like best about the job is the fact that no day is ever the same as the last. The worst part is probably clients who treat us like a supplier rather than trusted advisors.

'I didn't choose this particular career within advertising. I came to it by accident. I suppose it helped in one way because I had an open mind, which is a good thing. I filled in one application form that was available to anyone who asked, came for two interviews and got the job! In terms of qualifications, a good, solid degree helps.

'My advice to anyone facing an interview for this sort of job is be yourself – don't try and give them what you *think* they want. If you get the job by being fake, you either won't like working there or they won't like you. And if you don't get hired you'll never know if they'd have liked the real you more...'

SHARING YOUR CLIENTS' ENTHUSIASM

To be effective in helping the client meet their various objectives, an account handler must understand the client's business and have a real feel, even empathy for, the company and its philosophy. Why they do what they do. Why they don't do what they don't do. You have to be able to really get under their skin. It's about understanding their customers. And their rivals' customers. What's their motivation to purchase? What turns them off?

Sharing the client's enthusiasm is vital. Some clients get really passionate about the sort of things that most of us, hand on heart, couldn't give a monkey's about. He'd never tell you, but your client knows that the new toothbrush he's launching is dull. Deadly dull. Mind-numbingly dull. So do you. But unless you make it sound exciting to your creative team, the creative work is *guaranteed* to be dull.

Lindsay Cole, an account manager at a business-to-business agency, got to grips with her client's product in a practical way. 'I worked for a client that manufactured plastic plumbing systems. Not the most exciting thing in the world but we launched a really innovative new system that was especially fast to put together and install, and so saved labour costs. The copywriter and myself visited the factory and we spent a whole day there putting a hot water system together. It took us absolutely ages, and I'm sure we didn't do it right but in the end we got to know the product, what it did, and how it went together.'

GETTING ON WITH CREATIVES

One of the skills of a good account handler is being able to judge whether the creative work (which results from the interpretation of your creative brief) is right or wrong. And if it's wrong, why? And what can be done to make it right?

A company could advertise a new barbecue sauce a hundred different ways – so what makes a campaign featuring a single father any better than one featuring two mums in the kitchen doing the can-can, or even a talking sausage called Henry?

Unless you conduct consumer research on each campaign there's no right or wrong answer. What you have to be able to do is evaluate the creative work to see if, first and foremost, it answers the strategy and then ask yourself, is it creative and does it have any negatives? (For example, is the headline too subtle? Has a competitor run a similar campaign?)

Since creativity is so subjective, the account director often finds him or herself debating these issues with the creative team – either before the work is presented, or afterwards, when they're relaying the client's own comments and suggested changes back.

Depending on the egos of those involved, these issues may be easily resolved or they can be the cause of a shouting match and swift intervention by the agency MD or client services director.

This is where tact comes in. You'll be working with the same art directors and copy writers on other jobs so there's no point in making enemies. However, do stand up for what you believe in. If you're not fully convinced of the creative work, then how are you going to convince the client that it's right? Clients know this. Apart from smelling fear, they have an uncanny knack of sniffing out uncertainty.

All account handlers are known collectively by the disparaging term of 'suits', so they're at a disadvantage before they even start. For an account handler to be successful the creative department must see beyond the 'suit' label. To gain their respect you need to show that you're truly interested in the creative product, and not just in getting work approved by the client. Creatives like account handlers who are willing to take a risk on creative work. The campaign might be unconventional – even truly bizarre – but you don't mind presenting it. (Actually, in these cases, it helps to have a 'safe' option as well. You don't have to present this to the client – just have it with you as a 'Get Out Of Jail Free' card.)

You'll also gain creatives' respect by chatting to them about what they're doing (not just ads they're designing for you) and asking why they've done something one way – and not another. Even knowing which photographers are 'hot' can do a lot for your credibility.

Of course, the fast track to getting on like a house on fire is displaying an unnatural interest in football. That and beer.

PRESENTING TO CLIENTS

Presenting creative work (as well as media schedules and research reports, etc.) is a regular occurrence for the account director. Depending on the nature of the presentation, sometimes you'll have your creative director there. Sometimes you'll have your media director there. Both are experts in their chosen fields. But most of the time you'll be on your own or with your underlings. Presentation skills (and looking presentable) coupled with an overall knowledge of the market are, therefore, vital.

On a day-to-day basis the account director will usually be dealing with the client's sales and marketing director, advertising director or marketing director. Occasionally you'll have to present campaigns to the client's MD and possibly the board. You'll have to be able to present your ideas (and arguments) lucidly and forcibly and be able to provide convincing answers to questions like, 'Why is the headline in blue, not green?', 'Why aren't you using the *Daily Telegraph*. My wife loves that paper?', or 'Why can't the product photograph be twice as large?'

Some of your answers will be based on fact ('Because *The Times* has a better cost per thousand than the *Telegraph*') while some are subjective (the colour of the headline). That's where the client relationship is most useful. It enables the client to have trust in you and what you do, and therefore accept what appear to be (and what sometimes are) arbitrary decisions.

As an account handler, the ability to think on your feet is essential. So is having a point of view. Never ever say, 'I don't know'.

'I was once asked by the sales director of my client why we chose a particular typeface.' said one, an account director who wishes to remain anonymous. 'I had no idea of the process behind the decision but I knew it was a classical font. I told him that it gave the brand authority and endorsed the heritage aspect we were trying to promote. It did the trick and to be honest, I would have probably given the same answer whatever typeface we'd used'.

THE IMPORTANCE OF BUILDING THE RELATIONSHIP

It's when you don't have a good relationship with a client that things can start to go wrong. Accounts can be lost not because a client doesn't like you, but because he's indifferent to you. In this case there's no inherent loyalty to you – and therefore to the agency.

This is particularly important during reviews and pitches, when the value of a relationship cannot be underestimated. You're probably asking 'If the relationship's so good, why would the client hold a review of the business?' Good question. Sometimes, and particularly for public bodies or multinationals, there are statutory reviews. Sometimes a change in

management at the client automatically leads to a review (it's some sort of macho, Tom-Cat-Marking-His-Territory Thing) and in some cases, the client has no real intention of changing agencies; it's just done to keep the incumbent on their toes.

Of course, if the relationship's good, then clients are also more forgiving when errors do occur.

CLIMBING THE CAREER LADDER

As with most jobs in advertising, progressing through the various stages of account management is based on your ability. Occasionally (and just occasionally, mind you) clients have been known to pass compliments about the account handlers and their performance to the MD or client services director. That never does anyone any harm. That, and managing to persuade the client to spend more money year on year, are good ways to get ahead. There's no set period you spend as account executive or account manager. It's a question of proving your capabilities and having the right opportunities to take on a more senior role.

But what happens when you

reach the dizzy heights of account director (or senior account director, for agencies that are hot on job titles)? Well some are happy to stay in the position while taking on greater responsibilities as far as the size and value of their clients is concerned (and being rewarded accordingly). Being an account director on an multi-national piece of business can involve non-stop travel, visiting subsidiary agencies and acting as a sort of international trouble shooter (it sounds glamorous but the novelty wears off after four months).

Becoming a director is the next career move, but what about beyond that? Well, a high proportion of agency MDs were account directors. But if this degree of power isn't satiating enough, then there's always the option of setting up your own agency.

And should the time come to set up on your own, that close relationship with your clients means they're more likely to follow you.

GLOSSARY
● **Contact reports**
Also called contact records, these are minutes from a client/agency meeting which record decisions taken and responsibilities for taking projects forward.

● **Brand book**
Usually a ring binder, this contains marketing background information for the particular client – for example, media schedules, copies of current ads, competitive ads, research reports, the latest contact reports, timing plans, estimates etc., basically, anything that you'll probably need to refer to in a client meeting.

● **Billing**
The name given for invoicing a client at the end of each month. One of the more satisfying tasks of the account handler.

SKILLS YOU'LL NEED
A lot of stamina, superior juggling abilities and the wit, eloquence and flexibility of a true diplomat. You'll need people-management skills, communication skills for conveying briefs and sales skills to help sell your ideas to the client. You'll also require reasonable numeracy, a fine eye for detail and to be a good team player. If you can bring creativity to that heady mixture too, so much the better. Oh, and an even temper so you don't start laying into those lazy so-and-sos in the studio with a 2 by

4 the first time they let you down...

TIPS
● Read these sections:
Graduate Training Schemes
and **Other Routes into
Advertising**.
● If you're still wondering
about which degree to take,
consider something with
'Business' in the title. You'll
have a better grasp of the
world your clients are living in
– and they'll respect you more
for it.
● Be prepared to do the most
menial of tasks in your first
few weeks (or even months),
particularly at smaller
agencies. There's no shame in
this and you'll laugh about it
later.
● Make sure you get on with
all people at all levels.
● Never feel that account
handlers are superior to the
service departments within
an agency, like production
or traffic. They are not. One
account handler who talked
down to his production
controller could never
understand why his ads were
always the last to come out
of the studio – and why it
required him to stay until 8
p.m. most nights to approve
them...

ART BUYER

Money: £22,000+

Hours: 9 a.m. – 6 p.m. approximately but there's a tendency to work long or irregular hours if the job demands it. For example, you might be on a photographic shoot which takes you away from home for a week, or you might have to oversee some urgent retouching that goes on through the night.

Health Risk: 2/10. Pretty risk-free. You might accidentally trip over a cable at a photographer's studio or get a paper cut from leafing through a photo library catalogue but that's about it.

Pressure Rating: 7/10. The art buyer is responsible for making sure that everything agreed at a pre-production meeting is actually delivered. Responsibility also rests with the art buyer to make sure everything is sorted in terms of contracts and fees with suppliers.

Glamour Rating: 2/10 – 10/10. Depending on your status and the sort of agency you work for, there's the opportunity to go on exotic photo shoots round the world. (Don't get overexcited; most art buyers stay at their desks working out the budgets for these exotic shoots.)

Travel Rating: 2/10 – 10/10. As above, but only when you're established in the department.

The art buyer is to a press advertisement what a TV producer is to a TV commercial. Put simply, the art buyer is responsible for ensuring that all the visual elements that the art director or designer wants in the final ad are actually delivered – in time and on budget.

Working closely with the creative team and production or traffic person, they are responsible for commissioning photographers, illustrators, models and model makers according to the brief they receive. And then screwing them down on price.

Before you get too excited about this job, be warned that it's usually only the larger agencies which tend to have art buyers. In most agencies the job function is taken up by other positions in creative services such as production, traffic or even the

PA to the creative department.

That means it's a difficult area to get into, compounded by the fact that most agencies who have art buyers usually only have one or two. Don't be deterred by this. It's a great position – a job where every day is different and one that enables you to really get involved and have an influence on the creative process every single step of the way. What's more, you don't even have to know how to draw.

Although their main function is to source and recommend the right photographer or illustrator for the job, art buyers have to be tough negotiators when agreeing a price for the work. They then prepare a cost estimate for the job either for the traffic person, production person or account handling team.

Ben Cole is the head of art buying at HHCL. He got this position the way most people do, by working his way through production and traffic departments, taking on more art-buying responsibilities as he did so. He now heads a department of three.

Ben says, 'It's very rare that anyone joins an agency as a junior art buyer or assistant art buyer. While it is possible to move into this job from being a creative secretary, PA or photographer's assistant it's really best to have production or traffic knowledge so you understand the creative processes involved in producing an ad. It's a question of working your way up, looking for that opportunity. Before I started in production I worked in the post room. That's a very traditional route into this job'.

A junior in the department will spend a year or two calling in suppliers' portfolios, filing and sourcing library shots. After that they're usually given one or two smaller clients that they're more involved with, including organising photo shoots on their own.

A good art buyer needs to understand what the art director is looking for in terms of the content of the ad – and will know who can provide the expertise to turn a layout into reality.

Ben says, 'Every day I see two suppliers, it could be a photographer, an illustrator – maybe even someone who body paints. It's anyone that provides a creative service. I keep a huge file of samples of their work so I can easily source someone according to the particular brief I'm working to. If I can't think of anyone appropriate I'll phone a colleague in another agency, or search other sources like industry directories like the *Creative Handbook*.'

These are the sort of creative services an art buyer has to source:

PHOTOGRAPHY

While there are photographers who are jacks of all trades, there are more that tend to specialise in a certain area such as locations, portraits, celebrities, sport, architecture, food and drink or close-up work. The art director or designer might already have a particular photographer in mind – which makes life easy for you. On the other hand, they might tell you the sort of shot they want – for example, a famous marathon runner photographed in grainy black and white from the back of a moving vehicle. In this case you'd have to source a photographer who would be capable of taking this image to the desired quality.

LIBRARY PHOTOGRAPHY

It's bad enough when the client only has £500 in the budget and you need a shot of a sun-drenched St Lucia beach, but what about when the same client with the same budget wants a shot of the Earth seen from the moon?

It's quite simple really. There are loads of commercial photo libraries containing shots of virtually anything in the world (and beyond). You call them up, tell them the image you want and they'll send you a selection that the designer can choose from. (They usually also send in shots that are completely irrelevant but that's another issue...)

ILLUSTRATIONS

As with photographers, you'd be sourcing illustrators according to the brief – for example, whether you want an ultra-realistic airbrush illustration, a computer-generated image, something that looks like an engraving or wood cut, something done in pastels, a caricature, a technical drawing, a watercolour – the variation in styles is endless. There are a few large companies that represent a number of illustrators, each specialising in a particular style so a few phone calls will usually find someone who fits the brief. Equally, there are a vast number of freelance illustrators and commercial artists. An excellent source is an annual directory called *Contact*.

MODELS

Whether it's a beefcake or a busty blonde, someone who makes Rick Moranis look like Sly Stallone or a Henry VIII look-alike, finding the right model is also down to the art buyer. All professional models are represented by an agency and it's a matter of briefing them as to the sort of person you want, getting their portfolios in to show the creative team and possibly setting up casting sessions.

It's the same with animals. Want a monkey that can ride a bike? Or a rhinoceros that can ride a bike (OK, maybe you'll reach a dead end there)? There are companies that specialise in supplying animals and handlers for film and TV work who you'd need to contact.

MODEL MAKERS

If you absolutely, positively cannot find a rhinoceros that can ride a bike – and your art director won't take no for an answer, then model making may be your answer. Professional model makers are those people who were entranced by toilet rolls and sticky-back plastic when they were kids – and who now make a living doing the same sort of thing but on a far more sophisticated scale.

Although it's fun being involved on the creative side of things, being an art buyer is not without a high degree of responsibility when it comes to the legalities involved.

Ben explains, 'When it comes to commissioning photography, you've really got to be on the ball as far as things like **buy outs** and **usage fees** are concerned. It's absolutely vital that you know the full extent of the fees that are going to be concerned so that there are no surprises later'.

GLOSSARY
● **Retouching**
Enhancing photographs by adjusting the contrast or colour – or by adding or deleting elements. All clever stuff and all done on computers these days.
● **Photo library**
These are businesses offering commercial collections of photographs that ad agencies can use for the final ad itself.
● **Pre-production meeting**
Meeting between the creative team, account handlers and the art buyer where an individual project is discussed in terms of what is trying to be achieved creatively, what are the potential problems or concerns – all set against budget and

time considerations.

● *Creative Handbook*

An annual directory that lists contact details for suppliers of all creative services, from photographers to make-up artists, to companies that can translate copy into Bolivian – and everything in between.

● **Buy outs and usage fees**

The cost of hiring a model for a photographic session is usually based on the use to which the final shot will be put. For example, as with buying photographs themselves, the cost increases if the shot is being used over a long period of time, overseas or across a variety of media such as press ads, posters, on the Internet, etc. This might be uneconomic, in which case the art buyer and the model's agency would negotiate a buy-out fee. This is a one-off fee which covers unlimited use, but for a fixed period, say a year.

SKILLS YOU'LL NEED

The job of art buyer brings you into contact not just with suppliers but with all sorts of agency staff across all departments, and sometimes even clients. This means you've got to have the ability to get on with everyone. When it comes to dealing with creatives at a senior level, you mustn't be afraid to voice your opinions.

The job requires good artistic judgement, which is not necessarily something you can develop through experience, as well as plenty of enthusiasm and appreciation for art.

It's also vital to have an up-to-date understanding of the various legalities regarding usage rights, etc.

TIPS

● The best way to become an art buyer is to get in on the ground floor as a production assistant, gathering knowledge as you work your way through the department.

● Visit galleries, photographic exhibitions, subscribe to design and photographic magazines – any source of information about new techniques and new people. Start your own collection of these names and references that you can show at interviews.

USEFUL COURSES

While there aren't any actual courses that teach you how to become an art buyer, the London College of Printing offers a one-day course called **Picture Researching**. This provides a comprehensive introduction to the skills and procedures required including copyright law, reproduction fees, the use of Photo CDs and new technology and its implication.

For further details contact:

The London College of Printing
Elephant & Castle
LONDON SE1 6SB
TEL 020 7514 6770
WEBSITE www.lcp.linst.ac.uk

ART DIRECTOR

*The art director 'directs' how an
advertisement or commercial
should look. Using photography,
illustration, animation, model
making, typography, or any
other graphic element at their
disposal, it's the art director's
task to come up with the best,
most effective and creative way
to communicate a message. Oh
yes, and do it within budget.*

In simple terms, in an
advertisement the copy-
writer is responsible for
the words and the art director
is responsible for the pictures.

OK, as you've seen in the
section **How to Get into the
Creative Department**, that
was true up until a few years
ago. Nowadays it's much more
of a joint effort with the
copywriter and art director
working very much as a team,
pitching ideas for both the
visual and written elements.

That said, art directors have
the background in design,
which usually makes them
better placed to decide the best
way of communicating an idea
visually.

Don Beardsley has been an
art director for seven years and
works at St Lukes. He says, 'In

a traditional sense, the copywriter is responsible for the text in the ad and the art director is there to draw up the idea and to see it through the creative process of choosing the photographer or the illustrator, going on the shoot, supervising the retouching, etc.

'I work differently in what we call project teams. My partner is another art director; however, we both write. We both come up with the ideas. We both draw them up and we both look at the copy or the script. If it's an ad with long copy then one of us would write it roughly to start with, then we'd both refine it. If it's a big project, like a brochure, then we might draft in a freelance copywriter. By working this way you're a team within yourself. More agencies are working that way.

'We start by sitting down with the account director and the planner and discussing the problem together. There's no monopoly on a good idea and we'll all discuss various executions and probably throw a lot out. My partner and I will then go away and develop an idea'.

BUT HOW DO ART DIRECTORS ACTUALLY KNOW WHERE TO START?

They and any other creative person involved in the project will be working to a creative brief that's been issued by the account-handling team, and possibly also the planner, if the agency has one. This brief will also have been signed off by the creative director and the client.

This brief itself is a couple of sheets of paper (or several of them, depending on how complicated the task is) that provides the following information:

- Name of the client
- Name of the product
- Background to why the advertising is needed (it could be a product launch, to create awareness, to combat competition, etc.)
- Description of the product
- Target audience (who the advertising is aimed at)
- Main communication (what is the most important message that the advertising should convey)
- Supporting thoughts (what else needs to be communicated)
- Objectives of the advertising (it might be to increase awareness of the product, to

achieve a particular sales target, to win sales from a competitor, etc.)
● Tone of voice (e.g. professional, straightforward and ungimmicky; fun, funky and subversive)
● Media (e.g. 40-second TV commercial, half-page press ad, 48-sheet poster)
● Timing (e.g. ad to run September; first scripts required in June)

Since account handlers like impressing people with how much paperwork they can generate at any given time, this brief is usually accompanied by rafts of information about the product being advertised, including copies of competitors' ads, sales figures, research reports and all sorts of other dull stuff that creatives tend to ignore.

Getting a brief in this way happens in the ideal world. In smaller agencies where there might be fewer (or no) systems in place, the art director might find the briefing consists of a two-minute chat from the account handler who's between client meetings on a crackly mobile – or a few scribbles when he returns, presented on the back of a sticky Kit Kat wrapper.

Either way, from this information the art director will start thinking about the best way to convey the message from a visual point of view.

Just as there are many different ways to skin a cat, so there are many different ways to promote cat food.

Take a brief for a brand of cat food where the proposition is that 'cats find it irresistible'. Not the most original proposition in the world, we admit, but stick with it. Let's consider six different ways this message could be conveyed.

For starters, how about the safe option of a cat looking longingly at its owner who's about to open up a new tin?

Then there's a cat who's tucking into a tasty bowl of the stuff, impervious to a whole family of fat mice walking past it.

What about a cat that's gorged itself on so many tins that it's lying on its back, its paws on its belly with a big contented smile on its face?

Or a cat dressed up as a person (with a bad false moustache) at the supermarket checkout, trying to pay for a whole basket of the stuff?

Then again, how about a row of cats at the vets, all with their heads stuck in identical cans of the cat food?

And finally, what about the idea of a cat trying to reach a tall cupboard that contains the tins, teetering precariously on top of some home-made stilts?

There you have six different ways to convey the same message – and an even greater number of ways in which this idea can be executed. They could be photographs or illustrations. And if they're photographs, are they photos of real cats that have been retouched, or realistic models of cats? If they're photographs, what type of cats are they? Tabbies? Tortoishells? Siamese? Ginger Toms? Or what about one of those scary-looking hairless cats? And then there's the people in the shots. These will have to be cast from a model agency. Men? Women? How old are they? What are they wearing? What hairstyle should they have? Should one of them be hairless?

If we go for illustrations, are they in black and white or colour? Realistic or cartoon? And what about the headline for the ad? Does it go at the top of the ad or the bottom? Or how about the middle? Then there's the copy itself. Does this run above the headline, or below it? Or does the headline actually bisect the copy? Is the headline in colour? If so, what colour? And what about the typeface? Classic or contemporary?

And how about showing a shot of the cat-food tin in the corner (this is called the pack shot)? How big should it be? Should it be in the bottom left or the bottom right?

Decisions.   Decisions. Decisions. But decisions that an art director will have to make.

Once you and your partner think you've cracked the brief, you try and sell your idea to the account handlers and/or the planners (probably after presenting it to your creative director first). A good creative team understands that the account director and the planner know far more about their clients and their clients' business than they ever will. If the account director doesn't like the idea, then it's very probable their client won't either and it's no use throwing a wobbly about it. If they think that a witty pastiche of Troillus and Cressida is the wrong way to go on a TV commercial aimed at 18-year-old working-class males, then it probably is.

Really, you shouldn't have made the mistake in the first place, so there's no excuse for sulking or saying, 'Take it or leave it'. It's part of an art director's job to be 'hip' or at least to know what's hip. And that means not just understanding 'yoof' but 'Middle England' and just about everywhere else as well.

Once the idea is approved internally, it will then be drawn up to a degree of finish so that the client can understand what the hell the art director is talking about. It's rare these days for an art director to be able to draw convincingly so it's likely that a layout will be produced by either a visualiser or a Mac operator.

If the ad is approved then the choice of the photographer, illustrator or model maker will probably be the result of conversations between the art director and the art buyer.

Portfolios will be gathered and a decision made on the basis of who's 'right' in terms of ability, availability and cost. In the case of a TV commercial, the art director will choose a director and film production company on the same criteria, looking at their **show reels**.

The art director will brief the illustrator or photographer, and in the latter case, be present at the shoot so he or she can be on hand to make any last-minute decisions (like where the art director and photographer should go for lunch, for example).

The art director will choose the shot from all those taken on the day, decide what retouching needs doing and brief the studio that's going to do this – either the agency's own studio or an outside supplier.

When it comes to putting the ad together, the art director will brief a designer, or an artworker, or a typographer – or a combination of them (see the separate sections for these roles to see how they interact with the art director).

If it's a commercial, then the art director will talk to the director of the commercial and discuss his ideas for the feel, the look and any particular shots he has in mind. (The director will also have a firm view on the style of the commercial and might even make the majority of the creative decisions – with the consent of the art director.)

All in all, being an art director is a very varied and exciting job. You'd love to be one, wouldn't you? So would thousands of other hopefuls! If you haven't already done so, read the section **How to Get into the Creative Department** which shows just how fiercely competitive it is.

Don got into the industry by a conventional route. He says, 'I took a BA in Graphic Design at St Martins School of Art. In my final year I specialised in advertising. Although this gave me new skills in understanding colour and layout, the most important thing is the idea. It doesn't really matter how it's first presented.

'A copywriter came up to me at my degree show, liked my work and got in touch. We got our portfolio together, working up all our favourite ideas. We then went on a tour of the agencies to try and get a placement. The benefit of this is that you're able to work in a real agency, on a real brief. We did four placements before we got offered a job at BBH. I split up with my partner after two years and moved to my current job.

'My degree wasn't important in getting a job. Getting a job is all about showing you've got ideas – that's the most important thing. Free yourself up. Don't think about advertising or the way it's done. Express yourself naturally. For example, if you like humour then use humour. The most important thing is to demonstrate creative thinking. The execution can come later.'

In terms of what makes a good art director, Don says, 'You have to be original, creative and be aware of different graphic styles – what's in at any moment. You've got to be on the ball. Reading a lot helps. You've got to have a general appreciation of layout, what looks right, and a sense of attitude to your work.

'The worst thing for an art director to do is not be themselves. And if I'm looking for staff, the sort of people I look for are those who I think will frighten me for my job.'

Some art directors stay art directors, moving from agency to agency to work on bigger and more prestigious accounts. Alternatively, you can progress to the position of creative group head (supervising a number of creative teams) or head of art (responsible for all the visual design that comes out of an agency), or even (drum roll) creative director.

GLOSSARY
● **Show reels**
Copies of a director's recent (and/or best) commercials.

SKILLS YOU'LL NEED
You need to have a good understanding of design and layout but you don't need to be

able to draw (some of the best ideas can be jotted down using just pin men and kiddie-style drawings).

TIPS
● Look through previous copies of the *D&AD Annual*. This contains the best ads from the UK and around the world, as voted for by a distinguished panels of judges. Don't get jealous. Be inspired!

● Find a copywriter partner and work up your own portfolio of work to try to get a placement (see the section **How to Get into the Creative Department**).

● If you're looking for freelance work, try contacting freelance copywriters (you'll find them listed in *The Creative Handbook*).

USEFUL COURSES
● **The West Herts College Post-graduate Diploma in Advertising**
For full details of this comprehensive 30-week course see the section **Other Routes into Advertising**.

● **BA (Hons) in Graphic Design**
A typical course includes a common first year introduction to a wide range of design applications and ideas, followed by specialisation in design, illustration and (sometimes) advertising.

One of the most famous graphic design courses is offered by St Martins College of Art and Design.

For course information call St Martins on 020 7514 7022 or visit their website at:
www.csm.linst.ac.uk

The London College of Printing offers these short-term courses in design:
● Graphic Design: Introduction (4 weeks)
● Introduction to Professional Graphic Design (10 weeks)
● Graphic Design for the Printed Page (10 weeks)
● Designing Promotional Material (3 days)

For further details contact:
The London College of Printing
Elephant & Castle
LONDON SE1 6SB
TEL 020 7514 6770
WEBSITE www.lcp.linst.ac.uk

ARTWORKER (AKA MAC OPERATOR)

MONEY: £18,000 – £32,000+

HOURS: 9am – 6pm approx. Most artworkers work regular hours but some early mornings and late nights are not uncommon. It's very unusual for overtime to be paid. Freelancers, however, can work all the hours God gives them, knowing they'll be rewarded for it (before they get to heaven, that is).

HEALTH RISK: 3/10. In the olden days, when type was cut up by a scalpel and pasted onto a board, lacerations and accidental stabbings were pretty much an occupational hazard. Nowadays, eye strain and RSI from the keyboard are the greatest dangers.

PRESSURE RATING: 8/10. You're the last person in the creative chain before the ad or brochure or whatever reaches the production department and even a small artwork error can result in hundreds of pounds being wasted to put it right.

GLAMOUR RATING: 1/10. (Sorry, but spending all day sat in front of a Mac cannot, in any way, shape or form, be considered alluring or seductive.)

TRAVEL RATING: 1/10. (Unless you think that travelling from the train station to work and back again is particularly appealing.)

*As their title quite rightly suggests, artworkers – or Mac operators – are responsible for producing artwork on a computer for advertisements, posters, brochures, etc. These days this involves using **DTP** software to put the material into an electronic format that newspapers, **repro houses** or printers can use.*

One way to explain what artworkers do, and to show how they fit in with the other creative services, is to use a car analogy.

The art director might come up with the *concept* of a car with a removable roof, for use on sunny days and then *make* a car with this feature. To all intents and purposes this is a car. It has four wheels, an engine, instruments, seats, etc.

But, it's the artworker who has to make sure the engine is actually installed properly, that all the pipes, leads and wires are connected, that the steering wheel actually turns the wheels and the wheels go round – that sort of thing.

You see, an advertisement, poster, brochure or whatever, might look like the finished thing on a designer's screen, but there are many technical issues that need to be addressed before it can actually go to the newspaper or printer. There are also 'niceties' of design that the artworker can add to the finished project.

In most instances the artworker will take a design and 'artwork' it to the required standard and specification. In other instances (usually the more straightforward jobs, or **adaptations**), he or she will have more of a free rein on the design and will liaise with the art director, designer or typographer.

There are no hard and fast rules of how you work and how much freedom or influence you have on the design. It's all down to the individual projects you're working on and their own specific requirements.

Ryan Shellard is an artworker at Rainey Kelly Campbell Roalfe and says, 'I have quite a say in how the finished items looks but this does vary according to the job. A lot of art directors respect your opinion as they get too engrossed in the concept and don't have time to get involved in the finer detail.'

Projects tend to be allocated by the studio manager on the basis of workload and abilities. Some artworkers have particular skills in certain areas. Retail accounts, for example, need someone who's capable of high speed and accuracy (and not getting bored) while prestigious literature needs someone with a more critical eye on design.

Whatever you work on, it's important to note that you don't have to be a Mac wizard to be an artworker. Many people in the industry don't have any computing skills when they start, but learn on the job, starting as a studio junior. All right, this job might entail buying sandwiches for all the other Mac operators and getting ice creams for them in the summer, but everyone has to learn sometime.

Ryan came into the business 'accidentally'. He says, 'I wanted to be an architect and had a job lined up while I was still at college. The company went bust but I knew someone in the advertising business. I spent two days with them in the studio and thought, "I like this".

'I started as a conventional studio junior doing mundane tasks but I bought myself a computer and practised in the evenings at home. This way I got used to the programmes and developed my skills. In this business you really learn all the time and the more you do, the more skills you develop. While the basic design software we use doesn't really change, every now and then something comes out which gives you more capabilities, or lets you do something faster or more easily and you've got to keep up with this.'

All agencies tend to use the same design software, which means it's easy to move from job to job. 99% of them use Apple Macs that run QuarkXpress for page design, Adobe Photoshop for retouching and image manipulation and Adobe Illustrator for creating pictures and graphic images. A few artworkers use Macromedia Freehand as an alternative to Illustrator but they tend to come from the Southern Hemisphere and are regarded as odd (either because of where they originate from or their choice of software).

The two main ways you can become an artworker are by promotion from within an agency or by acquiring formal skills via specialist courses in software such as QuarkXpress or Photoshop. Many artworkers began their careers from jobs in the post room or production departments and there are even a few good artworkers who started off as dispatch riders for agencies. Some companies, including Rainey Kelly, have an active policy of promoting from within.

Agencies like training people up because they tend to have different studio working procedures in place and the smooth running of the department relies on these being adhered to. It might be something as simple as how work is saved and filed on the network or a particular way of preparing artwork for the production department. Either way, if it's not done according to the book, files can be overwritten in error or whole pieces of work can be lost.

Artworking is one of the few positions at agencies where it's common for freelancers to be employed. These might be people who pay a monthly rental for desk space and provide their own computer equipment, being paid an hourly rate for the work they do. In some agencies they are almost permanent fixtures, working there for months or years. (In some instances they get paid on a 'per job' basis, so that artworking an advertisement will earn them so much, artworking an eight-page brochure, a different amount).

Other freelance artworkers are registered with employment agencies who provide specialist creative staff. They get paid on an hourly basis.

Being a freelance artworker is a great life because you can choose how much (or how little) work you do, depending on whether you need the money or are just plain greedy.

Paul Evans is a freelance artworker from South Africa who works in London. Like many of his colleagues, he works for an employment agency that specialises in supplying creative services staff to advertising agencies on a short-term basis. 'The shortest period I've worked is one afternoon. I was actually taking a day off but I got a call at home from my employment agency to say that a design company needed someone to artwork some packaging in a real hurry. A deadline had been brought forward and they were short staffed. That was really unusual as most of my assignments are for a week or so. I once ended up working in an advertising agency for seven weeks on a huge project that involved working on press ads for an airline to run in about ten different countries'.

For Paul, the main attraction of being a freelancer is that he can pick and choose his own hours, plus the fact that by working at different agencies he can get good experience of a wide variety of projects.

Paul adds, 'From time to time I get job offers from agencies who want me to work there full time. I've done it twice but have always gone back to being a freelancer. I love travelling and this way of working suits me. It gives me the chance to earn some money doing a job I like, then go off for two or three weeks'.

As to what makes a good artworker, it comes down to two things: speed and accuracy. There's no point being fast if the work is wrong. Similarly, work that technically can't be bettered, but which took forever to produce is equally useless.

Paul says, 'As a freelancer, I never really know where my next job is coming from, so I have to make sure I'm really good at what I do. I want companies to ring up my employment bureau and say, "Can I have Paul for a week?" rather than "Can I have an artworker for a week?"'

Apart from being quick and accurate, artworkers must have an eye for design and the ability to tell whether something 'looks right' on the page. This is vital when artworkers have to work on adaptations of advertisements to different sizes, for different publications.

Paul says, 'One of the most common errors is being given a size of an advertisement which might be 200mm x 120mm. Normally, the depth is shown first but if the person who gives you the size doesn't know this, then all sorts of problems will arise. When I first started out I spent hours trying to make all the elements of an ad work in a tall, skinny area, only to find out later that it should have been the other way round. This meant I had to start all over again and the agency had to pay me twice in effect for the same job'.

Unfortunately, some quirky left brain/right brain defect has meant that artworkers aren't the best spellers in the world. That's why it's essential that everything they do is spell-checked before it's completed.

When artwork is complete, a colour or black-and-white laser proof is run off and signed on the back by everyone involved in it, including the artworker. Some agencies even insist that the artworkers sign that the work has been spell checked – and woe betide anyone if a **typo**

is found...

Some people are content to be an artworker all their life, progressing to bigger and better agencies where they have the chance to work on some really prestigious and high-profile clients, while others see it as stepping stone to a job in design or even art direction.

As the last link in the creative chain before the work goes to the production department, artworkers are under a lot of pressure to make sure everything's finished on time. Ryan says, 'You get used to it. If you're no good working under pressure then don't be an artworker. It's as simple as that. Even with the tightest of deadlines we manage to get all the ads out on time. It's amazing sometimes but we always manage to make it happen'.

Despite these sorts of pressures, the main attraction of the job is the same for all artworkers – the variety of the work. Ryan says, 'All the work I do is different. This week, for example, I'm working on press ads, posters and some stills for a TV commercial. To get a particular effect the director wants to film 750 separate pieces of artwork, 25 per second, and I've got to prepare them all!

GLOSSARY

● DTP

Desktop Publishing – a type of software that allows users to manipulate text, images and colour.

● Repro houses

Short for 'Reproduction' – companies involved in the various print processes like film and plate making, but not the actual printing itself. A sort of halfway house between the agency and the printer or publication.

● Adaptations

Different versions of the same basic ad design for use in different newspapers or magazines. The visual elements remain the same but these might have to be repositioned to fit a new size – e.g. a quarter of a page, a half page, a whole page, a spread in a magazine, etc.

● Typo

Short for 'typographic error' – usually a spelling mistake but it could be the wrong use of capital letters, punctuation, etc.

SKILLS YOU'LL NEED

In order to be quick and accurate, artworkers need to be very methodical and sticklers for detail. The ability to be focused and not easily distracted is vital, particularly because many studios have a radio or CD-player blaring in one corner. Forgetfully tapping the keyboard to 'Rockerfeller Skank' by Fat Boy Slim is just asking for trouble.

TIPS

● Get yourself a basic Mac set-up and software at home and learn the basics. You needn't have the professional software like QuarkXpress because this costs about £750. You can learn on simple DTP software like Microsoft Publisher to grasp the basics. (Most programmes work on the same principles.)

● Take a course to develop your skills as described above. Qualifications at the 'Beginners' or 'Intermediate' stages are recommended.

USEFUL COURSES

The London College of Printing offers some introductory courses for would-be art-workers, or those who want to brush up their skills. These are worth looking into:

● General courses

Absolute Beginner's Guide to Apple Macintosh (1 day) Introduction to Desktop Publishing (10 evenings or 6 Saturday mornings)

● **QuarkXPress courses**

Introduction to QuarkXpress (3 days, 10 evenings or 6 Saturday mornings)

Users QuarkXpress (3 days or 6 evenings)

Masterclass QuarkXpress (2 days)

Intensive QuarkXpress (1 week)

● **Adobe Illustrator courses**

Introduction to Adobe Illustrator (2 days, 10 evenings or 6 Saturday mornings)

Users Adobe Illustrator (3 days or 6 evenings)

Masterclass Adobe Illustrator (2 days)

Intensive Adobe Illustrator (1 week)

● **Adobe Photoshop courses**

Introduction to Adobe Photoshop (2 days, 10 evenings or 6 Saturday mornings)

Users Adobe Photoshop (3 days or 6 evenings)

Masterclass Adobe Photoshop (2 days)

Intensive Adobe Photoshop (1 week)

● **Macromedia Freehand courses**

Introduction to Freehand (2 days)

For further details contact:

The London College of Printing
Elephant & Castle
LONDON SE1 6SB
TEL 020 7514 6770
WEBSITE www.lcp.linst.ac.uk

CLIENT SERVICES DIRECTOR

 MONEY: £45,000+

HOURS: 12-hour days are common. So is entertaining clients, so be prepared for a few extra hours some evenings.

HEALTH RISK: See under **Account Management**.

PRESSURE RATING: As for **Account Management** but with the extra pressure that comes from the responsibility of having to sort out major problems across all the agency's clients, not just your own...

GLAMOUR RATING: 2/10 – 7/10. One day you're having a stale ham sandwich in a Bolton pub with the MD of a chain of bingo clubs. The next you're in a corporate hospitality tent at Wimbledon, entertaining the marketing director of a multi-national responsible for half the western world's supply of toilet disinfectant. It's a funny old life.

TRAVEL RATING: As above.

Client services directors manage the account-handling department and are also the people at an agency to whom clients go if they feel they're not being serviced or listened to.

They're there to nip problems in the bud before they develop into something much more serious that could jeopardise the long-term agency/client relationship.

If Henry Kissinger ever works in an ad agency (and who knows, he might) then this is the job he would probably do.

Client services directors are in a difficult position. They are responsible for the quality and level of account handling and, as such, have to acknowledge if the agency is underperforming and take the appropriate action to remedy this. Equally, they have to recognise if the client is responsible for a 'difficult relationship' and, if so, tell them. Either way, tact and diplomacy are essential.

If a problem does arise, the client services director is there to arbitrate, to consider both sides of an issue. They therefore have to display an element of independence.

To do this job effectively they have to get to know not just their own staff, but every one of the agency's clients, and have an overview of all their business and their key personnel.

Simon North is client services director at CDP. He says, 'My job is to co-ordinate across our client base and resources to make sure the right people are working on the right accounts for the right amount of time. It's all about the internal allocation of resources.

Simon says, 'I make a point to know all our clients at a senior level. On some, I know all the minutiae. On others I'm aware of the bigger picture but not the details. It's important to listen and quickly get to the core of a problem. Problems are generally easy to resolve and it's rare that something can't be sorted out. They're usually personality based and both parts of the relationship can be at fault. I'm a foil. People know I'll step in and try to take care of it.

'We operate an appraisal system, like a sort of parents' evening. This allows clients to talk to me about any concerns they may have. This is important because small niggles can hang around and if these aren't dealt with, they can become issues.'

As if the role isn't difficult enough, in most agencies the client services director will usually have, for historic reasons, his or her own account-handling responsibilities, which take up a fair proportion of their time.

Simon says, 'I reckon I spend 30% of my time as client services director talking to clients, 20% managing the account-handling department and 50% looking after my own business. On a typical day I'll start at 8 a.m. and will spend the first hour in internal meetings talking to people like the creative director or the head of TV about production costs. I have to make sure that I have a good overview of what's going on. Sharing information is important. I might meet the financial director or the new business director to discuss targets.

'From about nine I work on my own accounts. I'm responsible for about 25% of the clients at CDP. These are pieces of business I've worked on for a while, where maintaining the relationship is vital.

'Lunch is often with a client or I might discuss an appraisal with a colleague over a quick bite. Other times I'll have a sandwich at my desk and try to catch up.

'In the afternoon I might review some creative work with a team or discuss the brief and look at some possible solutions. Later I could be involved in a new business presentation or a brainstorming session for a client.'

The conventional route to becoming a client services director is by working your way up through the ranks of account handlers until you reach the heady heights of board account director and possibly head of account management. There's only one client services director, so opportunities don't arise that often. The main reason for people vacating this position is because they become managing directors elsewhere – or even start up agencies of their own.

The way Simon got into the business was unusual. He says, 'I was an army officer for six years and served in the Gulf War. That gave me the best management training in the world. I was 25 when I got back to Britain and I wanted to get into advertising. I sent my CV out and got 47 interviews in ten weeks. In the end I was offered three jobs including one as an account executive at CDP. I was working for much less than a captain's pay but stuck at it. I've been here now for nine years.'

He says, 'The best part about my job is the variety. Every day is different and every day is interesting. The worst bit is the hours. Twelve-hour days are common.'

With ultimate responsibility for the number and quality of new account handlers hired, client services directors almost drown under a wave of CVs every week as Simon can testify. 'I must get about twenty CVs a week and because of the volume we end up looking for reasons not to hire people. In covering letters it's important to keep up-to-date with developments and not make a reference, for example, to a piece of business that we might have lost or resigned two months ago. If you don't get on a graduate trainee scheme but want to become an account handler, my advice is stick at it. Keep sending your CVs in but pay careful attention to how they're presented. You'd be surprised at the number of people who even spell my name wrong. And that's simple!'

SKILLS YOU'LL NEED
To be an effective client services director it's important that you have an ability to listen and to arbitrate both internally and externally. You need to be a good communicator and, overall, a good number two to the managing director.

TIPS
● See the section **Account Management**.

COPYWRITER

The copywriter is responsible for coming up with the headlines, the text (the 'copy') and the **straplines** *in the case of press ads and posters, and the dialogue for TV and radio commercials. Now you know who's to blame for 'Chef's Square Shaped Soups Show How A Good Soup Should Be'.*

Copywriting is a misnomer.

Yes, copywriters write copy but they do a lot more than that. These days they play an integral part in the creative process, working with an art director, and possibly with a planner and an account handler, to come up with an original creative concept for an advertisement.

That said, they still write the copy or dialogue and the key to doing this successfully is not just in conveying the salient points that have to be communicated, but in capturing the correct 'tone of voice' for the ad. This is so the advertising message is credible and relevant for the **target audience.**

For example, the copy used to promote a Mercedes S-class should be authoritative, with gravitas, in keeping with the status of the brand and appeal to the buyers who aspire to this type of car. On the other hand, the copy used to promote something like the Ford Ka should be fun and funky, in keeping with the character of the car and the profile of its purchasers.

By the words used and the structure of the sentences, the copywriter will help set this tone. This can also be done by the amount of copy used.

Some ads have very little copy, making use of the visual and a clever headline to convey the message. Other ads have lengthy copy because of the creative approach. A series of ads for an Olympus camera a few years ago had a huge amount of copy describing what the camera did and the care that went into making and testing it. These ads were very successful. In simple terms, even if you weren't interested in photography and didn't give a monkey's about Olympus, just seeing a whole page of copy about the camera would probably make you think that it was quite a good make (well, if it was terrible, how could anyone write that much about it?)

But so they know what to actually write, copywriters work to a creative brief (see the section on **Art Directors** for more information).

So can you learn to be a copywriter? Well, yes and no. Providing you've got a basic grasp of literacy, it is possible to improve your writing skills by learning how to self-edit and be more succinct. One of the greatest skills is knowing when you've written enough – and when there's too much. But what's difficult to learn is how to think originally – and ideas are everything in this business.

Ideas can come anywhere and at any time. In the bath. On the train. In the cinema. Sometimes (but rarely) in the office. Most copywriters dwell on the problem for a long time, sort of sloosh it around their brain a bit and then let it percolate. Then, Eureka! A light bulb will go off and they'll scribble it down quickly before they forget it (the posh ones will make a note of it on their Palm V).

Vicki MaGuire is an award-winning copywriter at Ogilvys. She says, 'My advice to would-be copywriters is don't get hung up on English. It's the ideas that count. Ideas are everything. Don't worry about being good at grammar or spelling – that's what spell check is for. If it's a good idea then it doesn't matter if it's spelled correctly or not. You've got to have a good eye and a good ear'.

Vicki has been copywriting for eight years and now specialises in rebranding – giving tired brands a new lease of life – however, she actually started out as an account handler. She says, 'I got into the industry by pure fluke. I'd done fashion design at college in Newcastle but I couldn't really draw. I used to describe my creations using words instead. My work got me a job working for The Body Shop, designing posters for window displays. Someone came into the shop from an agency and liked one of them and asked who did it. At the time I didn't have a partner or a portfolio but got a job at the agency as an account handler. I stuck with this for six months but hated it. At the time I was copywriting charity ads for the agency in my spare time to get practice. I was then given an art director as a partner.'

Debbie Taylor is a freelance copywriter and got her first job after completing a specific advertising course. She says, 'I took an "Advertising Writing" course at an art college. This course had a reputation of being difficult to get onto and was recommended to me as one of the best of its kind in the country.

'In reality the course was actually no use whatsoever as it didn't prepare me for the realities of the job. I learned all about marketing and media but what it didn't teach was how hard you needed to work, how hungry you had to be and how to be original. It was an art college but we had no contact with would-be art directors. We were given briefs to work to by the college lecturers, but bizarrely, had to work on these on our own.

'Anyway, I left with a Diploma in Advertising Writing and my portfolio and got a job in a small healthcare agency. Not many people go into a specialised field like this so the salaries are usually better. I then moved to competitive healthcare agencies before working on press, posters and TV at First City BBDO. I left here a couple of years ago to go freelance and this way of life suits me.'

So apart from being able to think of original ideas, what sort of characteristics does a copywriter need to have?

Debbie says, 'I would say what a copywriter needs is a

butterfly mind. You should have a superficial interest in a lot of things. You don't need a deep understanding of the product you're promoting. You just need to know the basics as long as you understand the benefits you're trying to convey. Sometimes you have too much information and you've got to be able to separate the wheat from the chaff. You have to be quite ruthless with your own work and be good at self-editing. Don't be too self-indulgent and think in pictures as well as words.'

Vicki adds, 'As a copywriter you've got to be thick skinned and stand up to criticism. You'll be getting feedback from your creative director and clients so you can't afford to be too precious. But at the same time, don't be a pushover. Self-belief is very important and so is resilience. You've got to be able to bounce back after getting work rejected.'

If you're starting out as a copywriter, the most important thing is to practise. The more you write, the better you become. Most copywriters advise making up your own briefs and working to these with a self-imposed deadline. This isn't just to gain useful experience before you get a job.

It can be just as helpful after you've got one. Vicki says, 'As a junior copywriter you might end up getting all the crap jobs to do, which means your Book will look dull. Working up these spoof ads will really make it look a lot better. When you're next in the supermarket look around for brands that you haven't seen advertised for a while and invent ads for these products.'

Debbie agrees, 'My advice to would-be copywriters is don't bother with college. Get together with a keen art director and work on some ideas for ads together. Make up your own briefs and try to find a creative solution. Get a portfolio together and don't be too precious. If the art director comes up with a better line then use it.'

If you talk to a lot of copywriters, you'll find they're really passionate about what they do. Yes, it is difficult getting 'involved' in something like a microwavable organic lasagne or a new formula haemorrhoid cream, but the good copywriters can detach themselves from the everyday reality (and banality) and focus on the job in hand. For most, it doesn't matter what project they're working on; there's the same challenge of coming up with the Big Idea and crafting the copy around this.

Debbie Taylor says, 'The best thing about the job is the enormous amount of satisfaction I get when I know I've written a good headline or a good piece of copy, no matter who for'.

But ask a copywriter what they find most frustrating and they'll say it's the fact that copy is the first thing to be altered, with everyone from the account handler to the client thinking they can change it for the better. Debbie says 'The copy is the first thing to be changed. Clients will rarely tinker with the design of an ad but they feel they can rewrite copy. They'll edit one sentence in isolation and not refer to the whole paragraph. The problem is that everyone thinks they can write.'

If having your copy tampered with by these Philistines doesn't put you off, do you opt for a life of secure employment or one of freedom and flexibility? Debbie has done both but wouldn't go back to full-time employment. 'I prefer having freedom and choosing when I work and whom I work for but wouldn't choose this route if I wanted the camaraderie of a big company

and security of a regular pay cheque. These days I divide my time between copywriting for four or five agencies who use me on a regular basis, and writing on food and cooking-related projects for Waitrose. I used to be a chef so this is a particular interest of mine.'

As a copywriter you're rewarded and promoted according to merit, never on age or length of service. Good copywriters can progress from being a member of a junior team to a senior member of the department in just a few years. The really ambitious can aspire to be a creative group head (responsible for a number of creative teams), head of copy or even creative director. It's all down to you – and how creative you are.

But for many, copywriting is a stepping stone to another career which makes use of their writing skills. For them, writing ads is a way of earning a living from their particular talents until they can sell their best-selling novel, sitcom or blockbuster screenplay, make millions and spend the rest of their days beside a swimming pool somewhere *not* thinking of rhymes for 'Verruca' or catchy straplines for electric storage heaters. (That's one of the reasons why you'll be hard-pressed to meet that many full-time 40-year-old copywriters.)

Does this mean the job isn't as glamorous as people think? Well, it can be glamorous, depending on what clients you are working on and which media you're working in.

The sexy side of the business is the TV commercials, the posters and the national press ads. That's all well and good but there's a whole raft of other marketing materials that someone, somewhere has to write (it's a dirty job but someone's got to do it).

This material includes websites, mail shots, POS (Point of Sale) support material, in-store posters and displays. And then there are instruction manuals, newsletters and other forms of internal communications, plus corporate, product and possibly technical manuals. If it needs to be written, unless your agency is very specialised and narrow in the services it offers, then it's going to fall on you. That said, there are specialist copywriters in a lot of these fields. People who thrive on being able to explain the advantage between push-fit and solvent-weld plumbing systems, the technical nuances involved in trace heating – and that sort of thing.

But there is glamour to be had – for some lucky writers. In the 'old days' it was rare for a copywriter to go on a shoot. That was the remit for the art director. Nowadays it's more common for a copywriter to be there as well and have an influence on the art direction, or, in the case of a TV commercial, the post-production.

Vicki says, 'I know some copywriters who are never in the country. My opening lines for scripts are normally "open on white beach" but all my commercials usually end up being shot somewhere near Kings Cross!'.

GLOSSARY
● **Straplines**
A sentence or a few words that summarises the benefits of the product being advertised, or its desired positioning in the marketplace. Examples include 'The Ultimate Driving Machine' (BMW) and 'Reassuringly Expensive' (Stella Artois).
● **Target audience**
The intended recipients of the advertising.

SKILLS YOU'LL NEED

Above all, creativity and flexibility. You'll need to be capable of working in a wide variety of media, with a wide variety of styles, on a wide variety of products, many of which you won't be that enthused about. If you don't think you can come up with a new twist on the promotion of cheese straws or cough linctus, this probably isn't the job for you.

You don't need an in-depth knowledge of the English language, but knowing how to relate to members of a particular audience is essential.

For example, if you're writing for a youth market then it's important to know which words are 'in' and which are 'passé' right now, right this minute. Some copywriters swear that the only way to do this is to hang around the 'Two Ps' – the pub and the playground. We wouldn't recommend this. It sounds like a dangerous combination almost guaranteed to end in ignominious arrest and a good kicking in the cells to boot...

TIPS

● Find an art director partner and work up your own portfolio of work to try and get a placement (see the section on **How to Get into the Creative Department**).

● Try to get something published. Articles in newspapers or magazines. Short stories. Books. It proves you're creative. But don't think two film reviews in the Portsmouth Free Herald are going to cut much ice... aim high.

● If you're looking for freelance work, try contacting design agencies in your area. They very rarely have a copywriter on staff but may buy in services as and when they need them. The same is increasingly true of printers – even the high-street ones. They sometimes offer design services to their customers and may need someone to write that brochure on behalf of the client.

USEFUL COURSES

● **The West Herts College Postgraduate Diploma in Advertising**
For full details of this comprehensive 30-week course see the section **Other Routes into Advertising**.
● **The London College of Printing offers these short-term courses in copywriting:**

*Effective Copywriting for
Advertising (1 day or 6 evenings)*
This course covers how to think
of and express ideas to sell a
product, essential copy
elements, a review of good and
bad copywriting and an
understanding of tone of voice –
writing for different markets
and tastes.

*Promotional copywriting (1 day
or 6 evenings)*
This course covers the basics as
above, but looks at copywriting
for different promotional tools
including direct mail, posters,
brochures, leaflets and fliers.

For further details contact:

The London College of Printing
Elephant & Castle
LONDON SE1 6SB
TEL 020 7514 6770
WEBSITE www.lcp.linst.ac.uk

CREATIVE DIRECTOR

MONEY: £50,000 – £150,000+ Great creative directors are worth their weight in gold – and many get rewarded on this basis.

HOURS: How many have you got?

HEALTH RISK: 8/10. Although jet lag isn't terminal, a champagne and caviar diet can be.

PRESSURE RATING: 11/10. The reputation of your agency rests squarely on you shoulders. (Read this again if you're sure you want to be a creative director.)

GLAMOUR RATING: 4/10 – 10/10. In a large London agency you get a chance to meet the celebrity stars of commercials, and jet around the world filming them. And get paid. Lots. It's less glamorous working for a smaller agency, but you might meet an ex-BBC1 newsreader who's endorsing one of your client's products in a press ad.

TRAVEL RATING: 3/10 – 10/10. Whether it's international advertising festivals in Cannes, Milan, New York or Rio, the creative director will be there. You'll also be hard pressed to prise him or her away from TV commercial shoots in the Bahamas, Sydney, Singapore or Mauritius. In smaller agencies there's still travel, but usually not the kind that involves a passport.

With either a copywriting or design background, the creative director is ultimately responsible for all the creative work coming out of an agency – not just the quality of execution, but the quality of thinking as well. Agency reputations can be made or broken by this person. Just the personality and reputation of the creative director can often be enough to retain existing clients and attract new ones. How's that for pressure?

I t won't say this on your business card but in respect of the creative department at the agency you're the head honcho. The big enchilada. You're Da Man.

As creative director you're ultimately responsible for every ad, poster, TV commercial or piece of print work that leaves the agency. In theory that means you have to sign off and approve every single piece of work before it leaves the creative department, let alone the front door (although in practice that doesn't always happen).

You get invited to all the awards ceremonies, all the industry dinners and parties.

You can hire and fire at will. If you say 'jump' then your staff say 'how high?' You can go on as many exotic commercial shoots as you like. Clients respect you. Hell, even the agency management respects you. You earn a fortune and you get a damned nice car too.

Sounds good, doesn't it? Of course it does. The only problem is that there's only one creative director per agency. And everyone wants to be one. So how can you?

Well, creative directors earn their stripes by doing outstanding work in their field either as an art director or a copywriter. A good creative director must lead by example and inspire, and make everyone feel part of the team. This means that they have to be good managers and be prepared to get involved with the bureaucracy that comes with running the most important department in an agency. Not all senior art directors or copywriters want this 'hassle' and they are quite prepared to carry on designing and writing without aspiring to any headier heights. (To learn how to get a job as an art director or copywriter, read the section **How to Get into the Creative Department**. The individual roles are also discussed in detail in this book.)

As creative director, your day might include some or all of the following:

● Briefing meetings with planners and account groups
● Various internal meetings with agency management or department heads
● New business presentations
● Interviewing new talent
● Reviewing work with your creative teams
● Board meetings
● Sorting work to enter in competitions
● Judging work in other competitions
● Spending time with clients, getting to known their business
● Attending casting sessions, pre-production meetings or shoots
● Giving media interviews
● Oh yes, and designing or writing an ad or TV commercial.

Whatever size and type of agency, the creative director has the same remit, to uphold the standard and quality of creativity across all the work it produces.

Trevor Beattie is creative director of TBWA London, and

has been involved in some of the most innovative advertising for clients including FCUK, Pretty Polly, Nat West and Sony Playstation. He's been in the role since 1992.

He says, 'My job entails managing a creative department of some 50 souls, ensuring that the creative output of that department is of a consistently startling standard and acting as spokesperson for the agency to the media. There's also constant client liaison, the fronting of new business presentations and an occasional night's sleep. To do this job you need energy, enthusiasm, optimism, bloody-mindedness, self-belief, a thick skin, ambition and drive. Oh yes, no life outside work and Pinot Grigio.

'I love every single aspect of the job, well except the meetings, and that's why I'm still happily married to it after all these years. There's no such thing as a typical day. I don't really see work in terms of "days", it's more a continuous process of thinking, selling, explaining, drinking and never getting bored. Oh, and then sleeping.'

Like many of his creative colleagues, Trevor got his foot in the door after completing a degree in design. He says, 'I did a BA (Hons) degree in Graphic Design & Photography at Wolverhampton Poly. In my final year, I realised everyone else could draw better than me but my words were sharper than theirs so I started writing ads. My lecturer, John Lowe, put me forward for a placement at a large London agency against students from 50 other colleges. I still owe him. Anyway, when I joined Allen, Brady and Marsh on a 'creative scholarship' (I'm still on it) the ad world was a far more naive place. There was nothing like the ferocious rivalry and sky-high calibre of today's graduates.

'My advice to anyone wanting to get into the creative department is believe in yourself. Know what it is you have to offer the agency and industry at large. Be positive. Throughout my career I always acted like a creative director and one day someone made me one. Nothing changed. Academically, qualifications aren't important for this job but if energy and enthusiasm are qualifications you'll need a degree in both.'

Terry Carter is creative director at Adventure, a full-service agency in Sevenoaks.

He says, 'We have seven art directors and designers and I get involved with them in the initial thinking and then taking a more supervisory role as the ads are developed. I do a lot of presentations and tend to front the agency's creative resources in new business meetings and pitches.'

But what qualities should a creative director have, apart from the obvious one of being 'creative'? Terry says, 'You've got to have a good eye for what works and what doesn't. And good taste. You should never be too easily satisfied and should always look for opportunities to change something for the better even after the client has signed it off. I'm always looking to take our thinking that one step further and clients don't always understand that. They might be satisfied with what we do but that doesn't mean we can't improve on it.

'What's really frustrating is when you've put a lot of thought into something to make sure that the creative work is "on brief" and the client dismisses it without taking the proper time to consider what he's been presented with. How successfully you can talk through ideas with clients comes down to the chemistry with individuals and building up a rapport with them.'

Terry also got into the industry through his design background. 'I did a design course at college and specialised in illustration. My first job after graduating was in the publicity department of a local builders merchants. In fact I *was* the publicity department. I designed all their advertising in house and also booked the media. I then got a job at an agency in London in their artwork studio and while I was there the agency ran an internal competition to come up with new advertising ideas for Chanel. It was open to anyone. I entered and my ideas were chosen. Not a bad way to start really! I was there for seven years and worked my way up from art director to creative director, working on Cunard, Renault, the Royal Navy and Abbey National. After a spell running my own agency I was offered a job as creative director of a BBDO subsidiary and then moved to my current company about a year ago.'

Terry agrees with Trevor about qualifications. 'Formal qualifications aren't that important. What's vital is that you can demonstrate creativity not just in how you think, but in how you put those thoughts down on the page, or on the screen.'

The last word goes to Trevor, and his future career plans: 'To keep on keeping on. Then to rapidly get the hell out before I become one of the sad, malevolent, miserable old never-have-beens who continue to poison what should be a young persons' industry!'

SKILLS YOU'LL NEED
Apart from having a surfeit of imagination and energy, you have to inspire the creative teams in your department and push them to explore all possibilities on the projects they're working on. Equally, you have to be able to constructively criticise all the work you're presented with and show by example how it can be improved. Stamina and resilience are all important. It's a 24 – 7 job and you've got to be able to cope with the demands!

TIPS
● Read the section **How to Get into the Creative Department**, particularly how to get a partner and a portfolio of your work together.
● Also, check out the various vocational courses for art directors, designers and copywriters in the relevant sections in this book.

DESIGNER

A designer, or to give them their full title, 'graphic designer', is responsible for the arrangement of all the various elements on the page. These include form, texture, illustrations, colour and type.

It's the designer who gives 'shape' to the art director's concept (and then watches him or her get most of the credit).

Does the Ark of the Covenant exist? Is the lost continent of Atlantis buried deep under Antarctica? Where exactly does a designer fit in to the creative process?

Of all these questions that have plagued humankind over the ages, the last one is marginally easier to explain (let alone prove).

The first step in understanding the role of a designer is to distinguish between what an art director does and what a designer does. It's not that straightforward, as roles tend to blur a bit round the edges. Also, not all agencies have designers as such. All have art directors and artworkers (or Mac operators) and these positions are discussed in detail elsewhere. Where the position of designer exists, this is how he or she fits in.

Basically, it's the art director's job to come up with the general concept for an ad. For example, he or she might decide that the best way to promote a new brand of oven cleaner is to show miniature workmen chipping away at stubborn grease and grime with miniature pneumatic drills. (Actually, we rather like that concept – nobody pinch it, OK!)

Once this is agreed by the client then the art director would brief the designer on the idea. The designer would then go away and work up some visuals as to how the concept is best conveyed in, say, a colour magazine ad.

Some designers like to start off drawing **thumbnails** on paper, others like to design straight on to the Mac, and play around with layouts until they get something they like.

Whatever method is used, these initial layouts must contain all the elements required for the finished ad. This would include a headline, copy, logo, an illustration of the tiny workmen inside the oven and maybe even a coupon that offers money off the first purchase.

With all these elements to play with, there are probably hundreds of different combinations ranging from 'rubbish' to 'excellent', through 'truly bizarre'. A good designer will know by instinct which are the most effective and will concentrate on variations on these until he or she has a shortlist of a few which will then be worked up to a more finished state at actual size.

These will almost certainly have the headlines in position, along with the relevant photographs and will be correct as far as colour and size of type is concerned. At this stage though, they might not have the actual copy in position – probably because this hasn't been approved yet. In this case the designer will set the text in what's called 'Latin' or 'Greek'.

This is 'standard' text that's actually in Latin which starts 'Lorem ipsum...' No one knows what it actually means. It's there just to show the shape and size of the final type. And as for why this Latin is also called Greek? Just don't ask.

It's these layouts or visuals that will be presented to the client for approval.

At this point there are two schools of thought. Some agencies will have two or three layouts drawn up to present to the client, all of which will work creatively, on the basis that clients like to have a choice, and get miffed if they don't. This still means, however, that the designer can present his or her preferred option – using the others to show the evolution of the idea.

Others will just present one, on the principle of 'take it or leave it'. Of course, which method you follow depends on the individual clients and personalities involved. Even if one layout is selected, this might still have variation in terms of headline typeface, or the background colour – even if all the other elements remain the same.

Once one of these is approved, the job moves from the designer to the artworker, who's responsible for preparing the final artwork for production. But that's a whole other job title...

Designers at advertising agencies can work on a huge variety of projects: not only newspaper and magazine ads and posters but also a whole range of collateral marketing material such as brochures, newsletters, stationery, packaging, **point-of-sale** displays, **vehicle liveries** and building signage.

Simon Manchipp is Head of Graphic Design at HHCL and his work varies considerably. 'What I like best about my job is the scope of possibilities it offers. At any given time I could be developing the type for a TV commercial, designing posters, press ads, packaging or a new corporate identity. In fact, when I think about the job, there's nothing I don't like'.

Although this breadth of work means that designers have to be adaptable, the basic principles of good design remain the same. This means that both the message and the medium have to be taken into consideration. The rules governing the layout and size/amount of text in a poster, are far different from those in a **25 x 4** press ad.

Simon says, 'No matter what project you're involved in, what's vital is that you understand design and typography and can demonstrate innovative thinking. You need to be able to come up with the idea and be able to execute it. And because HHCL is such a collaborative work place it's important that you're capable of good people and presentation skills.'

Although it's true to say that some people do have a natural ability and an eye for graphic design, nearly all designers in an agency will have had some sort of formal training in the subject. This is because effective graphic design isn't just based on personal preferences and the random positioning of text and pictures on a page (despite what a lot of account handlers – and clients – might think). True, it might look random but in practice, the designer has made a number of decisions based on their understanding of things like the relationship of shapes and space, what attracts the eye, the study of colour and other design principles that have their basis on fact – not personal preference.

It's sometimes (sorry, often) difficult for a designer to explain to someone why, for example, the headline should be **ranged left**, or why the logo can't be twice its size, particularly when clients say something like, 'Look I'm paying for this space!' In these instances the designer has to be able to convince his critics (without losing his temper) that the decision was made for aesthetic reasons, and not on a personal whim. (Good luck in trying to convince a client of that.)

From their training, designers also know that changing just one element in the layout can lessen the effectiveness of the whole design – so that everything else has to be reconsidered. See, it's not as easy as it seems.

How did Simon get his first break? 'I took a graphic design course at a small college in Surrey and then took a graphic design degree at St Martins College of Art where I was picked up at my degree show by a design company. That's the conventional route into this business. It's very, very difficult to get in just by cold calling.

'Are qualifications important? Well, not really. What's vital is a stunning aesthetic eye for good design. After your first job it's vital to maintain a portfolio of striking and varied work which you can show to prospective employers. This is all I've taken to interviews. I've never actually been asked what my qualifications are.'

GLOSSARY
● **Copy date**
The deadline when artwork or film (known as 'the copy') has to be with the process house or the publication.
● **Thumbnails**
These are small sketches or layouts, so called because of their small size. These will give a general impression of the

layout without going into too much detail.

● **Point-of-sale**

Any graphic displays that you find in retail outlets, from a custom-made display promoting the latest MP3 players at Dixons, to a sign offering a two-for-the-price-of-one offer on toilet paper at Somerfields.

● **Vehicle liveries**

Applying a company's corporate identity to its vehicles through the use of type and a logo (or any other images).

● **25 x 4**

Press advertisements smaller than a page are measured by the depth (i.e. 25 cm) and the width – in this case, 4 columns of the newspaper. The column width varies according to individual newspapers.

● **Ranged left**

This means that the text on a page lines up along the left hand margin – i.e. the first letters on each line, align vertically. Other arrangements are 'ranged right', where the text on a page lines up against the right-hand margin; 'centred', where each line is centred on the page, and 'justified', where the text lines up on the left *and* right margins.

SKILLS YOU'LL NEED

It goes without saying that you'll need an eye for design and an appreciation of form, shape and layout. You have to interpret an art director's brief so, if you're not sure of anything, ask – never guess. You also need to have the courage of your convictions. If you really think your way of approaching something is better, say so.

TIPS

● When it comes to presenting your portfolio at an interview, it's definitely quality rather than quantity that counts. Having to leaf through endless examples of your work is not only time consuming for the person interviewing you, but is also extremely annoying. Include only the work you consider as your very, very best. Ten to fifteen varied examples, which show the range of your abilities, is probably about right.

● Keep your portfolio up-to-date and no matter how many people you hawk it round to, never give up. Design jobs are always hugely oversubscribed, but keep at it and, providing your work is good, perseverance will pay off.

USEFUL COURSES
● BA (Hons) in Graphic Design

A typical course includes a common first-year introduction to a wide range of design applications and ideas, followed by specialisation in design, illustration and (sometimes) advertising.

One of the most famous graphic design courses is offered by St Martins College of Art and Design. For course information call St Martins on 020 7514 7022 or visit their website at:
www.csm.linst.ac.uk.

● The London College of Printing offers these short-term courses in design:

Graphic Design: Introduction (4 weeks)

Introduction to Professional Graphic Design (10 weeks)

Graphic design for the Printed Page (10 weeks)

Designing Promotional Material (3 days)

For further details contact:

The London College of Printing
Elephant & Castle
LONDON SE1 6SB
TEL 020 7514 6770
WEBSITE www.lcp.linst.ac.uk

HUMAN RESOURCES MANAGER/DIRECTOR

MONEY: £28,000 – £50,000+

HOURS: Typically 9 a.m. – 7 p.m.

HEALTH RISK: 3/10. Low risk although stay away from dark alleys if you've just had to dismiss one of your staff. Particularly if he's six foot six and holds a heavy object and a grudge.

 PRESSURE RATING: 7/10. Lots of legal issues. Lots of financial issues. Lots of work. Lots of juggling.

GLAMOUR RATING: 4/10. Having to sit through a six-hour seminar on 'Organisational Change and the Aspirations of Middle and Line Managers' or anything remotely to do with pensions is not that exciting.

 TRAVEL RATING: 3/10. These seminars nearly always seem to take place in the Barbican and never Cannes or Florida.

Human Resources (HR) departments are responsible for managing staff, from hiring to firing and every stage in between. Finding the right people for the job, making sure they are happy with pay and benefits and responding to company policy and government legislation are all part of the job function. Remember, a happy worker is a productive worker!

It's been said that the assets of an advertising agency go up and down in the lift. That's right. Its assets are its people and only by the careful management and motivation of its staff can an agency hope to attract the best and brightest recruits and retain them. Agencies are notorious for poaching staff from their rivals, and clients can be quickly gained and lost when individuals or teams defect to competitors.

The administration of staff at all levels helps to ensure that staff remain contented in their jobs (even grateful for them!) which in turn should mean greater productivity and greater continuity of service.

However, while all agencies want to get the most out of their staff, not many have a Human Resources department. In fact, only the largest ones will, and often this department consists of only one or two staff members.

In most agencies the functions of a human resources manager or director will probably be taken up by a director responsible for recruitment and possibly training. Any contractual or employment issues will often be the remit of the accountant or financial director. In some agencies, there will be a personnel manager, but this role can vary greatly. Some personnel managers are just responsible for recruiting new staff, while others have a wider role similar to that of a human resources manager.

Although there might only be 120 – 150 individuals employed in this arena, it's a very varied and interesting career and suited for those interested in finance, the law but above all else, in people – and the difference they can make to an organisation.

Gaye Landau-Leonard is the founder of HRXcellence, a company that provides HR consulting services to senior management. She says, 'We advise them on how to attract the best talent, and then motivate, reward and develop this talent once hired.

'The component pieces of HR are recruitment, compensation and benefits, training and development, employee relations, employee communications, employment law and firing or disciplinary actions.'

The role covers such diverse topics as racism or bullying in the work place, personal development, pensions, team-working initiatives, alcoholism, work placement, appraisal systems, teleworking, changing job requirements, providing facilities for the disabled – anything that affects the development and performance of employees within the agency.

Niall Hadden is HR Director at WCRS. He's been in the role for about four years and each day is still different.

He says, 'It's a cliché but there's no typical day. Most days present a good mix of operational and strategic issues in these areas: employment law; policy formulation and implementation; reward management; resource planning and budgeting; training and development; relations and communications.'

Niall was instrumental in establishing the Human Resources department at WCRS but his background was in finance. He says, 'I worked for an investment bank in Dublin and then in a finance role at the Architectural Association in London. These two experiences contrasted greatly, traditional commercialism versus radical creativity. However, I felt comfortable in both environments and therefore thought that I would probably enjoy working in an industry where commercialism and creativity are fully integrated – i.e. advertising. I joined WCRS in 1994 as pay and benefits manager and gradually built this function into a fully operational HR service.'

Working in human resources means keeping up with the latest trends in people management and legislation, particularly relating to dismissing people and redundancy. One of the most challenging aspects of this work is balancing employees' interests with the interests of the company at large.

Gaye Landau-Leonard gives an example. 'Take dismissing staff. Often managers come to HR because they want to fire someone, which is fine except the manager may never have told the employee they are not doing well, and may never have put anything in writing. The HR person has to lead the manager through a fair process to improve the employee's performance, or dismiss them legally and fairly if that is the right thing to do.'

The same balance between employer and employee interests applies to rewarding staff. Gaye continues, 'When you're considering pay and benefits, HR people need to find that balance which allows a company to pay well enough to get great talent, but not *so* well that the company cannot afford its payroll. Creative benefits programs can help here, as can a merit system which only rewards top performers really aggressively.'

HR is definitely a role that's always evolving. Niall says, 'What I like best are the challenges that arise from constant change whether it's concerned with the organisation or new legislation. It's also interesting aligning HR policies to strategic business objectives and being in a position to influence and bring about change. When it's going well, the evidence is very visible.

'What I like least about the job is having to terminate someone's employment and the large volume of routine administration.'

The role though, does have

its lighter moments. Niall says, 'A candidate arrived in my office for an interview and before saying hello, asked me for a tissue to blow her nose. She blew her nose loudly and a bit chaotically, then gestured that I take the used tissue from her hand and place it in my bin. I was convinced that she must have been winding me up, but she wasn't. She was shown the bin herself!'

Because the role is so varied, so too are the characteristics that a good HR director should display. Niall views the following as important traits: 'common sense, numeracy, flexibility, the ability to think strategically and operationally, a desire to see fair play, an ability to deal with creative and non-creative people alike, an analytical mind – and rhinoceros skin.'

He feels that the worse traits are: 'indiscretion, impatience, tunnel vision, lack of attention to detail, oversensitivity, a preference for a closed door, an abrasive manner, fear of change and envy!'

Because of the relatively few HR professionals employed in the advertising industry it's not that easy to get in. It's easier to make the move from a finance role within the company. The professional body for human resources is the Institute of Personnel Development (IPD). It suggests that business studies, law and behavioural science are particularly relevant and offers a range of short-term training courses in management skills, personnel, training and development and employment law.

These are highly recommended by Niall. 'The most relevant qualification is the IPD graduate course. Personally I found this course invaluable. The good thing is that you can study for IPD qualifications at any stage of your career. I chose to do it by flexible learning through Malpas Flexible Learning, one of the main providers of this method of learning in the London and South East.'

Opportunities in HR are better at larger agencies and it is possible to move into the role, as Niall did, from related jobs within the agency such as pay and benefits manager or training and development manager.

Other routes in are via a position as a recruitment consultant, working for an independent employment agency or a headhunting company.

If a career in human resources is of interest then contact as many agencies as possible to see what opportunities exist. The difference in their ethos is often reflected in their approach and attitude towards human resources. Niall says, 'It's worth spending some time research-ing agency cultures in order to find the ones that might suit you best. It's quite amazing just how different they can be. Visit agency websites, examine their client lists and get as much publicity material from their marketing departments as possible.'

GLOSSARY
● **Headhunting company**
Headhunters operate in many areas of industry, including advertising. They select specific staff for specific roles because of contacts they have in different agencies or by word of mouth (they also never reveal their sources).

SKILLS YOU'LL NEED
Dealing with staff at all levels means that you'll need to be approachable, diplomatic, sympathetic, a good listener, compassionate and patient. The ability to remain impartial and not be influenced by emotions is also vital.

TIPS
● Contact the Institute of Personnel Development to find out about its courses, many of which can be taken while you're working. They also offer flexible learning whereby students are provided with coursework and study materials from an assigned tutor, and meet at a local support centre about once a month.
● Make sure you have the right personal qualities before pursuing a career in HR. These are as, if not more, important than professional qualifications required for the position.

USEFUL ADDRESSES
● **Institute of Personnel and Development**
IPD House
Camp Road
LONDON SW19 4UX
TEL 020 8971 9000
FAX 020 8263 3333
WEBSITE www.ipd.co.uk

IT MANAGER

Advertising agencies normally have complex IT systems in place to handle the transfer of data internally and externally, particularly computer-generated artwork.

It's the job of the IT Manager and his or her staff to oversee these systems and deal with day-to-day queries and trouble shooting.

It's common today for a lot of advertising agencies to outsource their IT services from a third party, although whether you work for one of these companies or are directly employed by the agency, the job is the same – to ensure the smooth running of the IT systems.

In all industries, these systems are important but in an ad agency they are absolutely critical. Because everything is geared around meeting deadlines, anything that interferes with the ability to supply images or artwork on time could have a very serious effect. What's more, the ability to handle international clients relies upon these systems being up and running 24-hours a day, 7-days a week.

In a simple case, a fault on

the **ISDN line** might mean having to spend a £100 on a courier to bike a CD from one side of the country to another. At the worst, it could mean an agency missing a deadline and wasting thousands of pounds on space that has been booked.

Thankfully, the latter case is extremely rare and there are back-up facilities and fall-back procedures in place to cope with problems and minimise the risk of these things happening.

Jeremy Harris is Head of IT at St Luke's and has three people in his team. 'In my experience the IT department tends to look after anything with a plug on it. We have to maintain the network and desktop PCs, train the users and look after all the different servers in a deep dark room in the basement. We also have to maintain the **firewall** to protect our networks and all the information they carry from the outside world. At St Luke's we're also responsible for maintaining the telephone systems, both land lines and all the mobiles including voice mail.'

Daryl D'Costa is the IT manager at a large London agency who also supervises three support staff. 'I'm responsible for keeping the computer network up and running and making sure all the PCs are functioning. If anyone has a problem or doesn't know how to use something then I'm the first port of call when there's a query, and the first line of support.'

In many cases, the IT manager can only identify the problem. If it's down to the software or a specific piece of equipment then it's the equipment vendor or the maintenance company that will probably have to remedy the fault. And while the Mac operator or account director becomes increasingly frustrated about why there isn't a ten-minute as opposed to a four-hour maintenance call-out contract, it's the IT manager who has to take the flak.

While being an IT manager at an advertising agency doesn't mean you need an intricate understanding of advertising, you do need an understanding of the professional needs of the agency. At one end of the scale, this will include their business philosophy and at the other, the 'kit' they use.

Daryl says, 'Most agencies use the same software,

Microsoft Office or the Lotus equivalent for word processing, presentations or spread sheets. They also tend to use the same e-mail and web browsing software. There are a number though, of specific applications for the industry. Things like integrated media booking and production and billing systems and also on-line data services. Things can go wrong here but it's down to the service providers themselves to solve the problem'.

Within the agency, the IT manager will probably spend the most time talking to the creative services director or the studio manager. This is because of the specific IT requirement of the studio. Although most Mac operators understand their equipment and can usually rectify faults themselves, the IT manager will be expected to be able to offer advice on the computers themselves, laser printers, scanners, storage devices, interruptible power supplies, **hubs**, CD writers, memory upgrades and even **fiery RIPs**!

Jeremy says, 'Looking after the equipment in the studio requires a different sort of knowledge. The machines they use are a much higher spec and that makes them more sensitive to malfunctions.'

In addition to solving problems, the IT manager might also have to establish new internal systems such as an intranet between companies within a group. And apart from dealing with in-house issues, the IT managers can often find themselves liaising with their opposite numbers at clients and suppliers in an effort to improve working practices between them. One example of this is the practice of agencies sending designs to clients for approval via e-mail, as pdf files perhaps, rather then posting colour proofs. In rare cases, they even allow clients to electronically amend these and e-mail them back! As far as clients are concerned, agencies have to make sure they're ahead of the game in the use of technology.

IT staff also find themselves getting more involved in the running and maintenance of agencies' websites, particularly if this involves dedicated password-protected areas where work can be posted for examination by clients.

In terms of starting out, it's harder to get into IT these days. The introduction and acceptance of the Internet, the growth in communications and remote working means there's a greater demand on IT staff both in terms of technical abilities and the qualities they must display. To get any sort of IT job, some form of recognised computing qualification is usually needed. As an IT manager it's common to have Microsoft or Novell Certification. These can be completed through part-time study if required.

Daryl has an engineering background but trained for IT because of the better job opportunities it provided. He says, 'The best part of the job is the relaxed atmosphere most of the day. I've worked at three different agencies and all tend to have a "work hard/play hard" philosophy.'

Jeremy gained his IT experience working at a local newspaper. He was there just as new technology was being introduced to speed up the print processes and developed his skills 'on the job'. As far as formal qualifications are concerned, he feels that while these are useful, experience and aptitude are just as important, as is an appreciation of the 'bigger picture'. He says, 'Technology is evolving so fast and it has to fit in with what equipment you already have.

To be a successful IT manager you have to be able to take a wider view and see how the introduction of one new piece of kit will affect every other aspect of the agency.

'We're there to offer IT facilities to as many people as possible. You have to be able to work in a demanding area and also fit in with the sort of people you'll be working with. You need to be good with people. It's all about wanting to help.'

GLOSSARY

● **Fiery RIPs**
An RIP is a Raster Image Processor – nothing to do with dreadlocks and everything to do with printing colour copies of ads.

● **Firewall**
An electronic barrier to prevent data being accessed by unauthorised parties, and to prevent infection by viruses.

● **Hub**
Think of it as a junction box for computers.

● **ISDN line**
High-speed digital phone line that allows the fast transmission of data. Agencies rely on this as much as on the normal telephone line.

SKILLS YOU'LL NEED

It's obvious really, but you must be familiar with, and enthusiastic about, technology, particularly the equipment used in a graphic studio. You should also enjoy solving problems and be aware of the latest developments. A knowledge of how an advertising agency works is also required in order to appreciate how technology is used within the company.

TIPS

● Target an advertising agency that has an in-house IT department.
● Be prepared to work your way up, learning with every new problem you encounter.

USEFUL COURSES

There are a number of ways of acquiring formal qualifications in IT including:
● **A-level** in Computer Studies.
● **HNC (Higher National Certificate)** in computing and IT subjects. These are part-time vocational courses, taken while you're working. There are many different types and it's best to check with a number of colleges of further education and higher education to see what courses they offer.

● **HND (Higher National Diploma).** Again, like HNCs there are a range of HNDs in IT-related subjects. Although these are usually full-time courses, some include work placements for a term, while others have a complete year in industry.
● **Degrees** relevant to the role of IT manager include Computing, Computer Science, Information Systems, Business Information Technology and Business Information Systems.

USEFUL ADDRESSES
● **National Training Organisation for Information Technology (IT NTO)**
16-18 Berners Street
LONDON W1P 3DD
TEL 020 7580 6677
WEBSITE www.itnto.org.uk

● **Computing Careers Yearbook** (London, VNU Business Publications, 1999)
Available free from careers services.

● **Institution of Analysts and Programmers**
Charles House
36 Culmington Road
LONDON W13 9NH
TEL 020 8567 2118
WEBSITE www.iap.org.uk

● **Institute for the
Management of Information
Systems (IMIS)**
5 Kingfisher House
New Mill Road
ORPINGTON
Kent
BR5 3QG
TEL 020 8308 0747
WEBSITE www.imis.org.uk

MEDIA PLANNER/ BUYER

MONEY: Media trainee/assistant £15,000 – £17,000; media planner/buyer with 1 – 2 years' experience £21,000 – £25,000; more experienced media planner/buyer £25,000+

HOURS: 10-hour days and 3-hour lunches. OK, that's the cliché about people who work in media departments, but there's no smoke without fire…

HEALTH RISK: 2/10. No one ever got hurt from booking a quarter page in the *Kent and Sussex Courier*.

PRESSURE RATING: 4/10. Negotiating and planning TV airtime can be a bit taxing but it's nothing to lose sleep over.

GLAMOUR RATING: 1/10 – 7/10. Being wined and dined at the top of the Oxo Tower by a national Sunday newspaper is cool. Having to sit through a 75-minute Powerpoint presentation from the publishers of a dreary magazine all about occupational health is not.

TRAVEL RATING: 2/10. Get cab to restaurant. Get cab back. Get cab to another restaurant. Get cab back. Get cab to a totally different restaurant. Get cab back, etc. etc. Lots of travel, but not that exciting.

Media planners are responsible for recommending where an ad, poster or commercial will appear and for how long, in order to be most effective. It's all about getting the right message in the right place before the right audience at the right time. (Now that's not too much to ask, is it?)

The best, most creative, most innovative, most staggeringly brilliant ad in the whole world is wasted if it's not seen by the right people. And that's where media planners/buyers come in. It's one of the rare job titles in advertising that's pretty self-explanatory. That's right. These are the people who strategically plan and book media.

Traditionally, media has meant newspapers, magazines, posters and radio, TV and cinema commercials. The growth of satellite and cable TV as well as the Internet has opened up brand new opportunities for advertisers and there are also some really quite innovative new ways of reaching customers via what's known as 'ambient media'. This includes things like ads on the backs of train and bus tickets, ads on petrol pump nozzles, on the fronts of supermarket trolleys, on milk cartons and even printed on the side of oranges.

Petra Osborne-Fardon is a founder of OJM (Osborne Jack Media) and explains the role. 'The planning process starts when we get a brief from the account handler. This will tell us about the product being advertised, why it's being advertised, when it's being advertised but, more importantly for us, who the advertising should be reaching. We call this the "target audience" and it could be any category of people. Depending on the product, we might be trying to reach people of a certain age, sex, class, geographic location, wealth – or any combination of factors.

'To find the best way of reaching this audience effectively, we look at media research. This includes published readership or audience surveys like TGI, NRS or BARB. These are regular studies of people's reading and viewing habits. We might also look at a competitive analysis so we can see where the client's rivals have been advertising.

'Once we've defined the audience and have decided the best way to reach them, we will put a plan together, weighing up options like coverage and frequency. Coverage is the percentage of the target audience that you reach and frequency is how often they see your ad or TV commercial. A good media planner will work within the budget to optimise these criteria. We do what we call "runs" to check our plans. These are computer programmes where we can enter different permutations of, say, magazines on a schedule, and different numbers of **insertions**. By adding or taking away publications or insertions, we can see the result this would have on the plan's effectiveness.'

But it's not just statistical information that's taken into account when planning media. The editorial relevance is just as important. Upmarket brands want to be seen in upmarket publications, and in most cases they are, because that's what their purchasers read. Being in the 'wrong' media environment will harm their reputation. That's why you rarely see an ad for Prada or DKNY in the *Daily Mirror*. Or *Men Only* for that matter.

The bigger the size of the ad (or the longer the commercial), the more the advertiser has to pay for running it. You also pay more for press ads that appear in colour. Position too, is important, and newspapers and magazines change premium rates for ads that appear in prime positions such as inside covers or on back covers.

The same goes for TV. A commercial that runs in the middle break of the news, or just before *Coronation Street* will cost an advertiser far, far more than a commercial that runs in the middle of some dodgy Channel 5 late-night film.

It's all based on audiences. In simple terms, the more people who see your commercial, or read your advertisement, the more it costs to advertise. The companies that broadcast the TV or publish the newspapers or magazines are known as the media owners, and they often quote 'cost per thousand' figures (cpt) – i.e. the relative cost of reaching one thousand of your target audience.

Once the media plan has been presented to the client (usually alongside the creative work), the media planner either becomes the media buyer, or hands over to the media buyer. Either way, they must now try to buy the planned **schedule** at the best possible rate. Unlike a lot of countries, media rates in the UK are negotiable. Newspapers, magazines and TV stations work off a rate card – this is their price list for selling space, whether it's a page in the *Daily Mail*, a half-page in *Pig Breeders Monthly* or 60 seconds within the latest *Morse* repeats.

It's up to the media planner/buyer to buy the schedule for less than rate card – as low as they can, in fact. Negotiating with the publications or the TV networks is one of the most important aspects of the job: about 80% of the buying process is done on the phone.

Petra says, 'Everything is so competitive today. Media is fragmenting and there's so much diversity that you need experience to negotiate a competitive rate. Clients need to see the savings you can provide them with, otherwise they might as well book the space themselves.

'Media has always been looked upon as second best to the creative work but now it's at the forefront. Clients are spending large sums on getting their campaigns placed and agencies have to be accountable.'

Media planners/buyers tend to work for two types of agency. Some work for the media department within a full-service agency, while others work for what are called 'media independents'. These are privately owned companies that are fully independent of an advertising agency. In reality, the job is the same. Media is big business and some media independents can be bigger than whole advertising agencies.

Richard Temple is a media planner/buyer at John Ayling & Associates, a media independent. He says, 'I was attracted to the job because of its variety and the early exposure to the decision-making process. It's very hectic and fast-paced. It's also very sociable as relationships are the currency of the whole industry. Media owners are not shy about entertaining media buyers they like and respect, but all relationships have to be managed, as you may find yourself having to tell media owners why they will not be getting business. Also, clients can be disappointed if they find that there is no availability for the periods they wish to advertise.

'My day's taken up by a combination of sales calls to media owners, dealing with client requests while trying to respond to service other clients. It's good working in a fast-moving industry. However, it can also be frustrating. There's often no time to stop and think strategically enough to solve a client's problem.

'To get on in this business you need to be well-organised, patient, strong-willed and have the ability to sell ideas. Oh yes, you need charm. No shrinking violets should apply. The job's a lot harder than I expected. My advice is don't join the industry if you're not prepared to work hard and work long hours.'

Petra likes the industry because of the amount of communication with a wide variety of media owners. She says, 'You always talk to new people and the diversity of the business keeps it interesting. One day you might find yourself booking media for a client whose total annual budget is £100,000. The next you might be negotiating on behalf of a client who's spending £20 million.

'On the downside there's a lot of administration, quite long hours and a lot of research to do. What's also frustrating is not being involved in the creative process early enough. That and getting poor briefs.'

Petra got her first job in media from an ad in *Media Week*. She started as a graduate trainee at a small media independent and worked her way up. She says, 'It's important to move around in your career to get plenty of experience of different agencies, both full-service and independents, and different clients.'

Traditionally, your first job in media agencies or media departments will be as a media assistant, helping experienced planners and buyers. You'll work on a portfolio of clients and most of the training is done 'on the job'. (Some large agencies send their new staff on training courses to learn more about media planning and buying skills.) After you've gained enough experience, you'll be given your own clients and will plan and negotiate on your own, although still working under the guidance of senior staff when it comes to the larger accounts.

Richard started in the industry by applying to a job advertised in *Guardian Media*. He used a recruitment consultant to find subsequent jobs at CIA MediaNetwork and then John Ayling & Associates.

He says, 'Some agencies will only take on graduates, but if you can overcome this arguable prejudice, then common sense, charm and a willingness to argue your point should get you into an agency. To succeed at an interview read everything you can about the industry. Be able to produce examples of media placements that you thought were good. Be prepared to defend your opinions.

'I'd recommend this job to anyone. Very few people enjoy their job in life. This is interesting as everyone you know engages with advertising and consumes media.'

GLOSSARY
- **Insertions**

Each ad booked within newspapers or magazines is known as an insertion.

- **Schedule**

A list of publications showing when ads will appear, and what size they will appear at – with costs.

SKILLS REQUIRED

In addition to being an effective communicator and negotiator, you must be extremely numerate; the sort of person who knows what 7% of 7 is* (this is one of the usual tests for numeracy). You should also work well in a team, have a wide knowledge of the media industry, be analytical, very computer literate and – you knew we'd say this again – be able to work under pressure.

TIPS

● You can begin a career in media as a graduate trainee. Although most agencies are looking for account handlers under these schemes, some positions in the media department are offered.

● There are recruitment companies which specialise in jobs in media. You'll find these advertising in the back of *Campaign* and *Media Week* – the media industry's weekly trade magazine.

● Some media planners/buyers start off as sales executives for media owners and then 'switch sides'. This can be a particularly good way to get in, as media owners are *always* advertising for new sales executives.

* In case you're wondering, the answer's a half (well, actually 0.49).

NEW BUSINESS MANAGER/DIRECTOR

MONEY: £20,000+ for new business assistant; £35,000+ for new business manager; £45,000+ for new business director

HOURS: 11 – 12 hours per day, but be prepared to burn the midnight oil as and when required.

HEALTH RISK: 2/10. Nothing to cause your GP (or you) any concern.

PRESSURE RATING: 5/10 – 9/10. The New Business Law states that 'the level of pressure is proportionate to the anticipated spend of the prospective client'.

GLAMOUR RATING: 4/10. There's a bit of the thrill of the chase about new business, but a lot of administration, research and reports to write – which aren't that thrilling.

TRAVEL RATING: 2/10 Don't worry if you don't have a passport.

This is the person who co-ordinates and helps implement an agency's search for new clients both proactively (i.e. by approaching prospects and marketing the agency to them) and reactively (i.e. by following up stories in the trade press about accounts which are on the move, real and rumoured).

When it comes to new business it's a dog-eat-dog world out there (although sometimes it's the other way round). You see, new business is the life blood of advertising agencies. They can't just rely on growing and prospering from getting more work from their existing clients. What happens if the MD of their biggest client suddenly leaves and his or her replacement has a best mate who runs another agency? Or if the client is bought by an international conglomerate which already has a good agency?

Although it's easier to gain business from existing clients (i.e. because the relationship is in place, they already know your work, etc.), not to go after new clients is suicidal. The 64 million dollar question is how do you get new clients? (And the even bigger question is how do you get new clients that spend 64 million dollars?)

That's where the new business manager or director

comes in. Most large agencies have one (or both), usually working as part of a new business team. Smaller agencies might not have someone dedicated to the task, but the role will be taken by a senior account director or possibly the managing director. However the agency is structured, and whatever the actual job title, the role is pretty much the same.

Emma Thwaite is new business manager at Leo Burnett and works within a team which includes a PR and Marketing Director and a new business assistant. She says, 'My role is to build relationships with potential clients on an ongoing basis so that when they are ready to consider changing agencies, Leo Burnett is front of mind.

'We identify and agree our new business plan at the beginning of the year. On a strategic level, I select groups of clients on the basis of their expenditure and/or gaps in our client list. I then market Leo Burnett to these people to raise awareness of us – who we are and what we do. I might send them **credentials** or a portfolio of our creative work. A lot of the job is **cold calling** or following up letters and mailings I might have sent them.

'On a tactical level, I have to react to leads in the trade press about clients considering changing their agency, or even drawing up a **shortlist**. I also work closely with influencers, mainly freelance new business consultants who are hired by clients to help them in the selection process of a new agency.

'I'm looking to build relationships with the prospective client at all levels of their company, over a period of time. The relationship could be ongoing for one or two months or for up to two years.

'All the time we're talking to the client and building this relationship, we're hopefully getting under their skin, understanding their needs and matching these to what the agency can offer. This means that when we do reach a stage where they invite us to talk to them, we can present something very relevant to them – and not just generalisations like, "This is Leo Burnett, this is our work and these are our worldwide offices."'

Clients change agencies for all manner of reasons. Sometimes they feel the agency is getting stale either strategically or creatively – or both. Sometimes they're right. Sometimes they might have a problem with one of the senior people on their business. Maybe a creative who's a real prima donna rubs them up the wrong way. Sometimes they change agencies because of a change in their own management. Sometimes it's because they're wooed by a rival agency's new business manager...

In any case, the process they usually go through is something like this:

Stage 1

They ask to see credentials from, say, six to ten different agencies who they think have the right profile for them (either in terms of size, capability, creativity, etc.).

Stage 2

They then whittle these down to a shortlist of three or four and issue each of these agencies with a brief for a project. These briefings normally take place face-to-face.

Stage 3

At an appointed time, usually over one or two days, these agencies will present strategies and creative work (including media proposals). This is known as the pitch.

Stage 4

The client will consider this work and based on subjective and objective reasons, choose a worthy winner! (Sometimes the creative work is tested in research groups before a decision is made. See the section on **Planners**.)

Tamarind Wilson is the marketing manager at Poulter Partners and also has responsibility for developing new business.

She says, 'My job is to raise awareness of Poulter Partners and our brand. We target those companies we want to have a dialogue with: those clients where we know we can add value. We have six areas of specialisation and have key prospects in each of them.

'Some clients feel uncomfortable if you get them in and make them sit through a whole formal credentials presentation. We like to get prospective clients in for an informal chat, or find out more about their business first so we can present a tailored approach to demonstrate what we can do for their particular business. We're one of the largest regional advertising agencies but we want to get people to think of us not as this – but who we really are and what we can offer.

'If a new client phones me up I'll direct them to our website. It's very advanced in terms of its technology and is WAP compatible. It also features a client extranet where our clients can privately access things like correspondence, artwork, photography, etc.

'I know that clients are extremely busy so our website is an easy way for them to find out a lot about us in advance. By providing this information up front the client can easily determine whether he wants to take the relationship further. We don't want to waste their time – or ours. It also means that clients who *do* meet us already have some sort of pre-disposition towards us, and are therefore better quality leads. I take the view that the more information you can provide to a prospect in advance, the more informed decision they will make. I'll be at this first meeting to find out what their specific requirement is and then introduce them to the relevant partner.

'This is a different way of doing things and the early signs are that it's very effective. Common sense and our experience with courting new clients shows us it's the way to go.'

But apart from marketing her agency to new clients, Tamarind also targets two other important groups. One of these is existing clients, so they can be made aware of what services Poulter Partners can offer; the other is staff. She explains, 'This is a very important group of people, which agencies tend to overlook. We have an internal body called the 'Ministry of Fun' which organises events. We encourage staff to socialise on regular occasions. We have summer, Halloween and Christmas parties and organise things like pub quizzes. Marketing the agency to the staff is just as important as marketing it to clients.'

In terms of what makes a good new business manager, Emma says, 'You have to be very organised and have an understanding of clients' needs. They are constantly being contacted by agencies either by cold calling or via mailings. It's a very cluttered market place and if you do enter into a dialogue with them, it's got to be relevant.'

Tamarind adds, 'You need basic marketing skills and knowledge but you've got to be able to work on your own initiative and be a good ambassador for the agency. Someone's opinion of us is important no matter who they are, clients, prospective clients, staff, suppliers or industry bodies.'

Tamarind got her initial marketing experience working for Hewlett Packard as a product manager, during which time she took and passed a sandwich course BA in Marketing at Huddersfield University. She made the switch to the agency side by getting a job at Poulter Partners, working her way up from account executive to account manager and then account director – working on Hewlett Packard there. She was appointed to the new position of marketing manager but still works on the Hewlett Packard brand, with a team under her.

Emma took an English literature degree and her first job was at a company called The New Business Consultancy. They provided an outsource new business capability and acted for agencies who didn't have an internal new business department. Emma worked there for two and a half years, acting on behalf of all types of agencies in London. She then moved to the agency side and Leo Burnetts is the second agency job she's had.

The entry-level job is new business assistant where a lot of your time is spent on research, putting documents together, compiling credentials and **show reels**. The usual progression is to new business manager and then new business director, ultimately responsible for the strategy and implementation of the agency's new business thrust.

The final word goes to Emma. 'New business isn't just regurgitating how good your agency is. It's all about giving clients a real reason to talk to you.'

GLOSSARY
● Credentials
Information about the agency in the form of a brochure or a video. This would include a bit about the company's history, its philosophy, its structure, key personnel, and most importantly, some examples of its creative work.
● Cold calling
Phoning or writing to a prospective client without any prior contact being made. A 'warm lead' is where the client already has some sort of relationship or connection with you, usually through a mutual

contact.

● **Shortlist**

When a prospective client narrows his list of potential agencies down to a manageable number, usually three or four.

● **Show reels**

A video of your best TV commercials.

SKILLS YOU'LL NEED

You have to be very organised about everything you do, and be a meticulous keeper of records. Resiliency and tenacity are essential, as is the patience of Job; some new business leads gestate for periods in excess of an elephant's pregnancy.

TIPS

● Vacancies in new business departments are not often advertised. To get in as a new business assistant it's best to get start as a secretary or PA and make your ambitions known to the new business director. Account handlers can also make the jump.

SPECIAL BONUS FEATURE!

Two innovative new business tactics that worked:

● Years ago an agency was pitching for the British Rail Account. The then chairman, Sir Peter Parker, went to the agency with his colleagues at the appointed time but was shocked to find an unkempt receptionist smoking a cigarette, chatting on the phone, and totally ignoring them. They sat down in a dirty reception area, litter strewn about, getting more and more impatient as the receptionist continued to ignore them. His patience finally exhausted, Sir Peter rose from his seat to walk out when one of the agency's senior management stopped him. Gesturing around him he said, 'This is how the general public sees British Rail. We're going to help you change that perception'. They won the business.

● On another occasion Saatchi and Saatchi were pitching for the Toyota account. They were shortlisted and on the day of their briefing at the agency's offices, the client was amazed to see a brand new Toyota in their reception area. To get it in they had taken out the whole of the reception frontage. The client was obviously taken aback by this gesture – but were even more impressed when they came back a few weeks later for the actual presentation.

This time there wasn't a Toyota in the reception. There were two. Guess what? The agency won the Toyota business.

NEW MEDIA OPPORTUNITIES

If you've been reading this book in a conventional manner (i.e. consecutive pages from front to back) you would have seen in the section **Types of Agency** that there are a growing number of agencies that specialise in new media, whether it's creating websites, banners or developing any number of e-commerce applications. This is good news because of the increased job opportunities.

Don't worry if you don't know your Java from your JPEG or your ISP from your PPP. Lots of people are scared off from applying to, or working in, new media agencies because they think they need to be really computer literate to get a job. That's not the case. What's important is that you have a basic understanding of the Internet and digital technology. Only programmers need to know the technical intricacies – and these aren't that difficult to master, as we'll see later.

This section does not attempt to go into detail about all the positions in these agencies. It's here to paint a general view of the different roles – what they do and how you get in. As for salaries, well it's difficult to pin these down. Account handlers tend to be paid about 10% – 15% more than their colleagues in conventional agencies. On the creative side, there's a big shortage of good people in the industry at the moment and if you can get in, it's a seller's market.

ACCOUNT HANDLERS

The job function of account handlers in these agencies is pretty much the same as in 'conventional' agencies – i.e. you act as the interface between the client and the agency. However, the main difference is that you are liaising with a much wider section of agency disciplines and external consultants.

Ben Harris is client Team Leader at Ogilvy Interactive (part of the WPP group) working on their Nestlé business. After taking a business degree he worked in the marketing department at PriceWaterhouse Coopers before getting a job as an account executive and then account manager at a full-service advertising agency. He says, 'I wanted to make the switch because the sector's really young, really new. There are loads of opportunities and the skill sets required link closely with advertising or certainly the ones picked up at my previous agency. I've always been interested in new media and am really self-taught, learning as much as I could about the industry and the applications in my spare time. I also taught myself to design and programme my own website.'

In his new role, Ben works at both a strategic and executional level. He says, 'First I co-ordinate with our consultants, planners, content architects, technical architects, designers, producers, copywriters and the account director to devise a European online strategy, which answers the brief. This means that I pull all inter-company resources and attend every meeting to do with this client, ensuring that everyone is briefed correctly and that every team member is on track, focused, progressing to schedule, and that the team is fully integrated and on brief.

'On a more detailed level, I have to ensure that we launch the client's website on time and on budget. For this job it has meant dealing with animation companies in Boston and New York (having daily conference calls and resolving disputes through negotiation), liaising with lawyers and editing legal documents, as well as sorting out hosting, security, tracking issues, data measurement, testing, artwork, production and design issues.'

To be successful in this field, account handlers should display the same skills as their equivalents in conventional ad agencies. Ben says, 'you've got to have a hard-work ethic and true determination. You've got to have a true interest in/knowledge of media and in particular new media. You need to have good management skills, an ability to prioritise tasks and to manage many different relationships at different levels. You also need to be able to come up with answers on the spot, to organise and be organised and have some writing ability.'

Ben's advice for anyone applying for his sort of job is, 'Make sure you've got a good all-round background knowledge of the industry. Relax, don't be nervous, be confident (not cocky), be yourself, express your passion, accept the invitation of a drink, don't spill it, and don't forget the fit has to be both sides.'

DIGITAL MEDIA MANAGER

Tom Hopkins is digital media manager at Brass Tacks, an online design company. 'I manage a department that's responsible for the design and implementation primarily of websites.

'Anything we do has to meet two objectives. There's what the user wants from the site they're visiting and also what the client wants – how does it want to be seen in the marketplace?

'We have people responsible for the design, the programming and account handling. There's also a 'techy' person on hand to help us out. We build the front and back ends of the websites. The front end is what the user sees. Apart from making sure the content is correct, it's giving the site the right look and feel, using the HTML programming language to create graphics to work with the site, and Java script or Flash to do any little tricks you see on screen.

'The back end is what we call hard-core programming. It's getting the server that hosts the website to send the right pages to the user at any time, sometimes using relational databases. This programming here is more complicated, using languages like Java script but also Delphi, Visual Basic and VB Script – and it starts to get into the realms of the geeky!

'I still design and programme, but less so these days. I'm more involved in running the department, overseeing the designers and programmers who work hand in hand to create and develop new media applications.'

NEW MEDIA DESIGNERS

A lot of people are put off from designing for the web because they think it's too technical. It's not, or at least it doesn't have to be. Some designers just design and leave it to the programmers to turn this into what appears on the web while others design and programme as they go along using HTML.

Tom says, 'As with most design, you need a good eye. The pages are designed in Photoshop so you obviously need to know your way around this software. Currently, a lot of magazine designers want to get involved in the Internet as they can see that's where the market's going.

'To get a design job at a new media agency it's absolutely

vital to have at least one website in your portfolio – even if it's your own which shows pictures of you and gives details of all your hobbies. You can design and implement a simple site in a day so there's really no excuse not to do this.'

PROGRAMMERS

These are the people who turn the design into reality so that it appears in digital form on the web. Many of them start their jobs as testers, looking at programming code, dissecting it and seeing what makes it work. They can then use this knowledge and little tricks and tips they've picked up and apply it to the work they're doing. Many more, though, are self-taught and Tom says, 'I don't think there's a real advantage in taking a computer science degree any more. The industry's changing so fast that what you learn can be out of date by the time you start work. Also, these courses tend not to teach you the programmes that industry uses. A lot of programmers don't have formal qualifications; it's quite easy to pick things up and there are a lot of 'teach yourself' books available. I've taught a secretary to use HTML in two days and a week later she had the

necessary skills to get a job as an HTML programmer.

'Programming web pages is a very satisfactory job as you can see the programme happening right in front of you, and you make adjustments which are instantly visible. In other more general programming applications you're a cog in the machine and what you do is only part of a much larger, lengthier process.'

SKILLS YOU'LL NEED

For working in new media, in whatever function, you've got to be interested in the Internet and e-commerce; what it can do and where it's going. It goes without saying that you can't be technophobic and since the majority of new media agencies tend to be quite small, you must be flexible in terms of your responsibilities and job function.

TIPS

For job opportunites in new media look in the recruitment sections of these magazines:
- *Revolution*
www.revolution.haynet.com
For subscription details call 020 8841 3970
- *Creative Review*
www.creative-review.co.uk
For subscription details call 020 7292 3703

● **The London College of Printing offers these relevant short-term courses:**

Introduction to Multimedia
(3 days)
Basic Multimedia Production
(3 days)
Introduction to the Internet
(1 day or 4 evenings)
Introduction to Website
Production (2 days or 4
evenings)
Website Production;
Introduction to Frontpage
(2 days)
Website Production I & II
(1 week each course)
Designing Killer Websites
(3 days)

For further details contact:

The London College of Printing
Elephant & Castle
LONDON SE1 6SB
TEL 020 7514 6770
WEBSITE www.lcp.linst.ac.uk

PA
(PERSONAL ASSISTANT)

As a PA (Personal Assistant), you're the boss's right-hand man (even though nearly all PAs are women). You're there to organise their professional life and sometimes also their personal one, usually because the former impacts so much on the latter. You have to make their day as easy and hassle-free as possible, so they can get on with the job in hand – running their business. It's part secretary, part confidante and total dedication.

It's difficult being a PA to someone. It's not that the job is over-onerous or the hours are extraordinarily long but it's a role where you have to put your working life on hold for someone else. You're responsible for organising your immediate boss – not yourself.

From a personal point of view, being a PA also puts you in an awkward position within the company. Some people see you as the eyes and ears of the director, MD or chairman you're working for and therefore treat you with suspicion. This can mean that you only get to know people on a superficial level.

These days it's more difficult to define what a PA is. Today's bosses can be far more computer literate and quite often do their own correspondence and deal with the day-to-day paperwork, which actually limits what a PA has to do.

The main and most important function, however, is organising their diary. Some bosses have two – one for social and one for business engagements. It's reported that Robert Maxwell had six PAs, each looking after a particular aspect of his life – and he expected them to be on call at all times. Thankfully, PAs in advertising have an easier time of it.

Annabel Lucas is PA to Paul Simons, the Chairman and CEO of the Ogilvy Group, a job she's had for ten years. 'My biggest task is keeping Paul's diary and co-ordinating all his travel arrangements. He has a driver who I brief every day, making sure, for example, that he has enough time to get from one meeting to another. I also arrange his meetings, co-ordinate the different departments and the usual secretarial duties like sorting out the post and answering the phone. The most difficult task I've had to do was when I worked with Paul at our last agency. I had to organise a reunion of 150 people who had worked at Simons Palmer going back eight years. I managed to track down every single person, apart from the odd temp!'

Kate Garrod is PA to Kate Percival, Chairman of the AMD Group, which includes several companies providing advertising, PR, corporate and web design, media planning, magazine publishing, and studio services. She says, 'Kate does most of her own correspond-ence but I might top and tail the letters. I also work on a lot of new business presentations or long reports for her. My other main task is looking after her diary, passing messages on and implementing anything that arises on a day-to-day basis. When I arrived, the group's corporate identity was in the process of being changed and I had to co-ordinate this with all the group companies to make sure this went smoothly and according to plan. My other main task was working on the new agency handbook, again liaising with all the departments to make sure this was correct and up-to-date.'

A few agencies want PAs educated to degree level but they tend to be in the minority. Most people become PAs after progressing through a range of secretarial jobs. In Kate's case she moved to London from Oxford and enrolled at St James Secretarial College on a six-month full-time course. This taught her speed writing, typing and interview techniques but also included a business studies course that covered all aspects of working in a commercial environment including company structures and what to expect in 'the real world'.

Her progression to PA was quite rapid. 'After I left college I joined a computer business as a team secretary. The sales director I was working for was made managing director and I became his secretary. I took voluntary redundancy when the company relocated and joined a financial printer as PA to the MD. He had been brought in by the American parent company to rebuild the UK operation and I was very involved in helping him do this. In the end I even had my own PA!'

After a stint as a PA at an intelligence company run by ex-SAS and military intelligence personnel, where discretion was the order of the day, Kate joined a PR company as PA to the owner. She says, 'It was great. I had my own office with a terrace. The company grew and grew and I became involved in a lot of recruitment. It was good seeing people I'd interviewed as graduate trainees progressing through the company. The company was eventually bought by Ketchum, but by that time it was too big and had lost that personal touch. I saw my current job advertised in *The Times*. I'd never worked for a woman before but I think they make the best bosses.'

Annabel's progression to PA was also fast. She says, 'I started out as a receptionist at an advertising agency by answering an ad in *Campaign*. I learned to type at evening classes and progressed to being a receptionist/secretary. I then became a secretary to an account director and then got the job as PA to Paul when he was chairman of Simons Palmer. I followed him to Ogilvys when he was appointed as chairman here.'

In terms of what makes a good PA, Annabel says, 'To be an effective PA you have to start with good secretarial skills. You've got to be organised and a good communicator, be honest, have an outgoing personality and be tolerant. You've got to be very discrete as your job usually includes your being entrusted with a lot of confidences. You've also got to have the ability to manage egos because of the seniority of a lot of the people you come across! Don't be afraid to ask for advice. There shouldn't be the need for guesswork in anything you do. Things are too important for them to go wrong. Be honest and upfront with your boss and try to make his or her day as easy as possible. Remember to be your own person and don't lose your personality.'

Kate agrees. 'You've got to be extremely diplomatic, organised and be extremely discrete about what you hear and see. I got good practice at this while I worked for the intelligence company where I had access to some extremely sensitive information. It's also about keeping that balance between being friendly with staff yet forceful enough so that when something needs doing, it's done right away.'

As all bosses are different, so is the length of the working day. Annabel says, 'Although Paul usually works a thirteen-hour day, I work a 40-hour week and I don't take work home with me'. Kate tends to work from 8.30 a.m. to about 7 p.m. in the evening but despite the hours, likes her job. She says, 'I've always wanted a role where every day is different, where the opportunities are up to you and what you make of them. Being a PA gives you this opportunity. You also get a much better knowledge of how the whole company works. It's good to get involved this way.'

SKILLS YOU'LL NEED

Many PA roles include some responsibility for client presentations so proficiency in Powerpoint (or similar) is a must. The most important character traits are being organised, a good administrator and being able to act on your own initiative so that you can run the office when your boss is away. You'll also need to be a good communicator at all levels including senior personnel at clients. Being smart at all times is also a requirement. As PA, you are representing your immediate boss and have to look and act as professional as he or she does.

TIPS

● Secretarial training is a must, often to 'executive secretary' level. If you're a secretary and want to be a PA, be interested in everything the agency does and not just your department, so you can get a full picture of the business.

● There are more opportunities to get a job as a PA by moving companies rather than internal promotion.

● *Campaign* magazine usually has a good selection of PA jobs at the back of their recruitment section.

PLANNER

MONEY: £35,000 – £45,000+

HOURS: 9 a.m. – 7 p.m. is about average for the industry. However, be prepared to attend **group discussions** some evenings (usually 7 – 10 p.m.) which might also involve an overnight stay.

HEALTH RISK: 2/10. The greatest threat to your health is probably enjoying too many sandwiches and crisps while attending a group discussion.

PRESSURE RATING: 8/10. Although time scales for projects are quite long, the pressure on a planner is being able to come up with The Answer. In addition, the effectiveness (or not) of the advertising usually rests on your shoulders.

GLAMOUR RATING: 4/10. Although planners work closely with account handlers, they sadly don't tend to enjoy the same lifestyle. If overseas travel is part of the job, then while the account director and client enjoy a night on the tiles in Frankfurt, the poor planner is probably observing a group of forty-year-old Hausfraus talking endlessly about vacuum cleaners. That or sandwich makers. Or detergent.

TRAVEL RATING: 2/10 – 8/10. Research groups are carried out in most of the main cities in the UK and Europe. Depending on whether you work on a national or pan-European account you might find yourself in Birmingham and Manchester – or, if you're lucky, Brussels and Madrid. It's unusual for a planner to travel outside of Europe (apart from when they go on holiday).

Planners, or account planners (or strategic planners, if you're really posh), are responsible for making sure the communication within an advertisement or a campaign is effective. They do this by developing the strategy and the brief that the creative teams work from, using their knowledge of the consumer to guide the creative work.

It's all very well devising creative work to meet a brief but how do you know it's going to be effective?

Planners are there to help ensure that the advertising *does* have the desired effect and they do this by overseeing and scrutinising the creative work from a consumer's point of view – before it reaches the TV screen or the printed page.

As a concept, planning (like sensible lunch times) is relatively new to the advertising scene. It was introduced in the late 60s and at the time, had its critics. Even today there are agencies that are very cynical about its function, seeing it as over-intellectualising the creative process, and an obstacle or a hindrance to good, original work.

But don't worry. Most large agencies have planners and place a high degree of value on their input. Richard Huntington, a planner at HHCL who has worked on Iceland, Tango and Texaco, describes his function like this: 'The creatives ask, "Is the work good enough?" The account handler asks "Will it happen on time and in budget?" while the planner asks, "Will it work?"'

The whole creative process begins with the creative brief, the single most important piece of paper in an agency (apart from the notification of your bonus). The planner writes this, with input from the account director.

This document is the first major step in making sure the advertising is effective. Here, the planner sets out not only what the advertising should be saying – and who it should be saying it to – but also why the consumer should believe it in the first place. This means the planner must understand the consumer's beliefs and motivations – what drives them and how this can best be communicated in a credible way.

How is this done? It's the result of the planner distilling mountains and mountains of research, current market knowledge, results of previous campaigns and his or her own insights. And if there isn't sufficient research in the first place, then the planner will commission new studies as required through a number of external research companies, each of which might have expertise in a particular area – for example, children, food and drink, high-tech products, etc.

To be effective as a planner you must understand the **target audience** and the market place in which your client operates, not just now, but in respect of future trends as well. This information might come from **desk research**, or from a specially commissioned study. However, nowadays clients have greater in-house resources and they compile a lot of this information themselves. This means that agency planners have to bring something different to the table – a true insight into what consumers think and want.

As Richard says, 'Now clients are capable of conducting their own research, which means that all clients and all agencies tend to be researching the same sectors and proving the same information. Before planning there used to be equality of ignorance, now there's equality of knowledge.'

At the end of the day, if the advertising is judged as being ineffective – for example, it didn't raise awareness, change opinions or increase sales, or all three – the planner usually carries the can. (It's the planner who also evaluates the effectiveness and has to recommend how future campaigns can be developed in the light of these findings.)

To be an effective planner you need to have a really good appreciation of the creative process. You also need to be articulate so you can explain clearly what might be wrong with the creative direction and how it can be improved to ensure that it's 'on strategy'. Oh yes, and you have to be a born diplomat to deal with all those creative egos along the way.

Richard started his career in advertising as an account handler in a direct marketing agency before taking on a planning role in a different agency. This is a typical route into the job, but it is possible to start as a planner straight away via one of the graduate trainee schemes operated by the large agencies. Some people become planners after working at a research company, although the need to have a research background is less relevant these days.

Many people who go into planning, either directly or via an account-handling role, have a degree in sociology or even psychology but this isn't a prerequisite. A lot of agencies seem to prefer people with a wider experience so you might find someone from outside the industry who worked initially as a management consultant, a solicitor, a marketing manager, or any number of other professions that involve working closely with members of the public.

In the planning department, the entry-level job is junior planner and you tend to progress to planner and then planning director. Some agencies also have positions for board account planners. As a junior planner you'd be working with a senior colleague, basically crunching data, attending research groups and gaining experience in **quantitative** and **qualitative research** skills over two or three years.

After this period you'll probably get autonomy on a small client, while still being supervised on other pieces of business. Most planners like the work because it gives them the chance to really think a problem through and be involved at the very beginning of the creative process. As with most jobs in advertising, every day is different. It's also one of the jobs in an agency where most of your day is spent thinking rather than doing.

Richard describes a typical day: 'Most of my time is spent in various meetings with the account director and creative team, developing and honing ideas for different clients. Between these I'll probably continue writing a brief I've been working on. I might also brief a research company or compile market data for a client on a particular area of their business, say, the soft drinks market in Northern Ireland.'

So what makes a good planner? According to Richard, 'Apart from having an appreciation of the creative product it's all about having an analytical mind and being able to consider lots of information, assembling the data and drawing conclusions from it. You have to be logical, but as you develop a strategy, you learn to think laterally which can put a unique spin on a brief. You've got to be enthusiastic and be able to inspire the creative team into producing their best work. It's about turning a really good idea into a great one.'

GLOSSARY
● **Desk research**
Existing published research that is in the public domain – for example, research companies might commission a report into what consumers think of washing machines, supermarkets, glue, or any number of different items. This is then made available (for a fee) to anyone who wants it.

Other desk research includes statistics or information found on the Internet or through news clippings, government statistical data, and textbooks – basically anything that's already been published.

(Don't laugh but a research study was actually

commissioned into glue and not surprisingly, the report began 'Glue is not an emotive issue...')

● **Group discussions**

One way of establishing consumer attitudes to something, whether it be a product or service, or even the advertising itself (to test its effectiveness), is by getting a sample of your target audience (see below) together and getting a discussion going with them. This is usually arranged by an external research company who will recruit your audience, provide them with refreshments and act as moderators in the discussion.

These can take place at someone's home, or at a viewing facility where the planner, the account handler and possibly the client, will secretly observe the group in session from behind a two-way mirror, or via a remote hidden camera.

This enables you to observe their reactions first hand (plus you can make insulting or provocative gestures without fear of being punched – although this is highly unprofessional, it must be stated).

● **Qualitative research**

Research that establishes what consumers feel and think – for example, do they think that Fairy Liquid is expensive? Do they think it lasts longer? Do they care about washing up liquid in general?

● **Quantitative research**

Research that results in pure statistical analysis – for example, the number of people who have heard of Fairy Liquid, the number of bottles they buy in a month, etc.

● **Target audience**

The consumers the advertising is aimed at. This might be young men, housewives, pet owners, married couples, single parents, etc. – subdivided into age range, geographical location, income, sexual orientation – or any number of other criteria.

SKILLS YOU'LL NEED

A planner often finds him – or herself having to inspire the creative team so it's vital to be enthusiastic about the product and the campaign every single step of the way. You also need an appreciation of creativity, an ability to think intelligently and logically, to be systematic, well-organised and persuasive. It's also useful to have the kind of lateral thinking skills that make Edward de Bono look like a clot (OK, maybe that's an exaggeration but you will need to be able to think laterally).

Above all, a planner needs to have a total understanding of their target audience and a respect for them.

TIPS

● Check the ratio between account handlers and planners. Agencies that take planning seriously have a 1:1 ratio. Some agencies just have one or two planners who are used in new business pitches only. Find an agency where the ratio is good, otherwise you'll acquire just superficial knowledge.

● Read the series of books called *Advertising Works*. These are case studies from the IPA Advertising Effectiveness Awards and give a unique insight into how the planning was conducted, the influence this had on the advertising, and how the effectiveness was evaluated.

PRINT BUYER

These are the men (and women) who are responsible for specifying and overseeing the printing of a vast range of promotional material, often used in conjunction with advertising campaigns. This could be literally anything – from a simple four-page leaflet to promotional beer mats, from car stickers to a life-size cardboard cut out of Chewbacca. And everything in between.

If knowledge is power then print buyers must be omnipotent. You see, printing's not just about putting ink onto paper. It's about knowing all about what sort of inks and what sort of paper.

But that's just the easy part. There's also considerations like **drying**, **varnishing**, **folding**, **stitching –** and that's not even thinking about the different printing processes in the first place – **letterpress**, **gravure**, **litho**, **screen printing**, **digital printing**. Not forgetting printing using designs cut into potatoes.

Print buyers need to have amassed a whole load of technical knowledge so they can advise on the best – and most economical – way to produce something, as well as ensuring that the finished result will be of the highest quality.

However, the nature of the industry means that technologies are changing all the time and the print buyer needs to be constantly up-to-speed with these developments.

Some of this knowledge comes from reading the trade journals like *Print Week*, *Print World* or *British Printer*. Other information comes from the printers themselves and other suppliers you work with, or trade exhibitions. It's not unusual for print buyers to receive a whole brochure from a paper manufacture telling them about a new range of papers. To you or me, these samples all look the same but a print buyer will caress and fondle them, paying attention to the grain, the sheen, the texture, as if handling some rare work of art that's been unseen for hundreds of years. (Yes, they should get out more.)

Jason Heaver is a print buyer with ten years' experience who works at the agency Brand Evolution. He says, 'Although a lot of the knowledge comes from on-the-job experience, nowadays you really need some degree of formal training. A lot of print buyers also go on training courses off their own backs so they can keep up with changes in the industry. The

technology is moving so fast, and people and processes are being removed from the printing process, driven by the need to produce materials to a high quality but to tighter and tighter deadlines.'

So apart from amassing all this technical knowledge, what exactly does a Print Buyer do?

Well, a typical day might include receiving briefings on a wide variety of jobs. Then there are meetings with reps from print companies who are at the agency to either deliver work, collect work or bend their ear with 50 reasons why they should use their company – despite the fact that the agency already uses eight other suppliers, all of which provide a good, competitive service, thank you.

In Jason's case it's a bit different. 'I have my own rosta of printers that I use and I'm just too busy to see reps who are cold calling unless I've heard extraordinary things about their company or they've got some amazing new piece of equipment. My regular suppliers just come in when I need them.'

A good part of the day would be in drafting specifications and sending these out to different suppliers to get the most competitive quotes. Then there are costs received from suppliers that need to be checked in order to determine who will get the work. (The cheapest quote might not necessarily be the best one. Quality of work and speed of delivery are also key factors.)

There will be the usual invoice checking, and sometimes arguing with printers over costs for amendments – like who's at fault, the agency or the printer. Or both.

Then there might be **proof checking**, or visiting a printer to look at a job as it's being printed. Jason says, 'The larger and more complicated the job is, the more important it is to see it being run. I see about a third of the jobs I handle on machine. I'm there to ensure quality control, to make last-minute adjustments to colour if required and to check any changes that the printer might have been asked to make.'

At the end of the day, print buying is a very varied job because no two printed items are ever the same. You might get similar shapes and similar formats but each job is different, with its own problems. Jason says, 'What I like best about the job is a sense of achievement. You get

involved at the beginning of a job and see it right through until you've got the finished, printed version in your hand.'

Jason received a grounding in basic print theory at a Media and Communications Study course at the Brighton College of Technology. He says, 'Soon after graduating I saw an ad in my local paper for the job of a production assistant at a Brighton advertising agency. I'd only been in the role for a short time when my production manager left. The first thing the managing director said was, "You know a bit about production, don't you? There's the department. If you need me, I'll be in the office next door". I found myself managing the studio and traffic departments and when the production director eventually left, I took over his job as well. After I'd gained enough experience I got a job at my current company.'

Working your way through the production or traffic departments, and picking up vital experience along the way, is the most common way to reach a position as print buyer. You should make sure though, that the agency you work for does handle a fair amount of print in the first place.

As an assistant print buyer

you'd be more involved in the administrative side of the business, like sending out jobs for specification and evaluating quotations. You'd probably also handle the smaller, simpler jobs under supervision. Print buyers have full responsibility for the spec and quality control of all the jobs and depending on the structure and size of the agency, might aspire to become production director. This person isn't involved in projects on a job-by-job basis, but is concerned with developing and implementing the strategy for how the production department is set up and how it operates.

But whether you're a novice or experienced, you use your knowledge to ensure that the finished product is 'fit for purpose'. This means that the print buyer has to start off with a correct specification in the first place.

You wouldn't print a prestigious brochure on the card usually reserved for cereal boxes. And neither would a '0% Finance!' window sticker for car dealerships use the adhesive normally found on car clamping warning notices (well not unless you wanted to travel round 600 Fiat dealerships with a razorblade painstakingly scraping all their windows afterwards – before using it on your wrists).

Okay. These might be obvious but what about printing posters to go in something like Woolworth's shop windows? Sunlight affects the pigment in red ink, causing it to fade, so 'light-fast' inks have to be specified. Then there's the problem with printing large areas of blue. Again, due to something in the pigment of blue ink, it never actually dries. Yes, it might look dry but unless it's sealed, the blue ink will rub off, on to the page opposite. (Tricky things, these inks).

Like most things in an agency, accurate briefs are needed. Only with a good brief, can the print buyer ensure the specification is correct. You know what they say about bad briefs – Garbage In: Garbage Out. But in the case of buying print, the rubbish could be very expensive rubbish – for example, 80,000 brochures that are 5 mm too wide to fit an envelope, because no one mentioned at the time that they had to be posted...

That's why it's vital for the print buyer, the designer and the account handler to all sit down at the beginning of a job to make sure that everyone knows the purpose of the job, the budget (if there is one) and the delivery date.

It's no good designing something that looks brilliant, that the client absolutely, positively loves, that is within budget – if it needs special paper that comes from one factory just south of Helsinki, and which has a delivery time of 6 – 8 months.

Oh yes, if you eventually become a print buyer, don't bother asking or complaining about why there's never enough time to print the damn thing, whatever it might be. There just isn't. All right?

GLOSSARY
● Digital printing
A relatively new method of printing where toner or ink creates the image on paper. Think of it as a super-duper ink jet or laser printer. Very useful for quick, short quantities.

● Direct mail
Basically, any printed material delivered to your door either by post or just posted through your letterbox, from a simple leaflet telling you how cheap it is to borrow £80,000 over five years, to a free trial offer of a dull periodical (and the chance to win £250,000 or a mystery free gift in to the bargain).

● Drying
Sufficient time has to be allowed for the ink to dry properly before a printed item can be folded, bound, or packed. If it's not, then a print buyer will describe the printing as being 'off set'. (You and I call it smudged.)

● Folding
After the job is printed it has to be folded to suit the final specification. Some weights of paper have to be scored beforc folding. Others don't. Some 'crack' if they are folded against the grain and are too dry. And you thought folding paper was straightforward?

● Gravure
Used for very long runs, like magazine printing. The image to be printed consists of thousands of tiny 'cells' etched into a plate that's wrapped around a huge cylinder. The ink is applied to these cells and is transferred to the paper as the cylinder rotates.

● Letterpress
Printing in Ye Olden Days and now hardly used at all – except to recreate what printing looked like in Ye Olden Days. The image is formed by ink being applied to raised letters or images on a printing plate.

● Litho

This process is used for the majority of printed items for short, medium or long runs. The image is printed from ink applied to a flat plastic or metal plate either on separate sheets ('sheet-fed') or on a huge roll of paper ('web').

● On the run

Term for checking something actually being printed – as opposed to checking colour proofs before the job actually gets on to the printing press. This is the last time you can spot errors – and hopefully do something about them.

● Proof checking

Before something is physically printed, the print buyer will see a colour proof. This is carefully checked for colour and quality and is then circulated around the agency for checking by anyone else associated with the job – and ideally the client. Only when it's returned to the printer, signed-off, can the job actually be printed.

● Screen printing

The printing process formerly known as 'silk screen'. This method forces ink through a mesh stencil and is used for printing on glass, plastic, fabric, metal – any material, of any size, in fact, that can't go through a conventional printing press (well, not without breaking it).

● Stitching

The industry calls it 'stitching' but we call it 'stapling'. Two stitches means two staples. Don't ask why.

● Varnishing

To make sure a large area of ink, like in a photograph, doesn't get 'off set' (see above), a coat of varnish or sealant is often applied. This also gives the photograph a slight sheen.

SKILLS YOU'LL NEED

As a print buyer, it's not only vital to keep abreast of the latest technology and advances in paper, inks, finishing, etc., you've also got to have a great memory to retain all the information you've amassed. It's also very important to be able to work under pressure and on your own initiative.

Oh yes, being able to function well after large amounts of alcohol can also be handy given the number of lunches that printers are wont to offer to induce you to use their services.

TIPS

The London School of Printing offers two short courses relevant to print buying:

● **Appreciation of the Printing Processes (5 days)**

This course provides a basic technical knowledge and appreciation of the processes involved in print. Subjects covered include colour scanning and film proofing, paper selection, print finishing, binding, folding and digital printing.

● **Print Buying and Estimating (3 days)**

As its name suggests, this course examines the implications of various printing processes on costs including creating and understanding specifications, production techniques, quality control and contractual issues.

For further details contact:

The London College of Printing
Elephant & Castle
LONDON SE1 6SB
TEL 020 7514 6770
WEBSITE www.lcp.linst.ac.uk

PRODUCTION CONTROLLER/ MANAGER

MONEY: £15,000 – £20,000 for production assistants; £20,000 – £30,000 for production controllers; £30,000 – £35,000+ for production managers

HOURS: 9 a.m. – 6 p.m. The hours tend to be pretty regular but late nights are sometimes required to meet urgent deadlines.

HEALTH RISK: 4/10. Those lunches offered by suppliers can be a bit damaging on the old liver.

PRESSURE RATING: 7/10. So many ads to clear and so little time.

GLAMOUR RATING: 2/10. Sorry. No one does this job for the glamour. For the suppliers' lunches maybe, but definitely not the glamour.

TRAVEL RATING: 2/10. As above.

Production controllers are responsible for making sure all the press ads that an agency produces get out to all the right newspapers at the right size and at the right time. They're also responsible for the quality of reproduction. (Not a job for the colour blind.)

The newspaper advertisement for that new brand of extra-length toilet tissue is ready at last. The copy's been written. The photography's been taken and the layout's been finalised. What's more, the creative department, the account handlers *and* the client all love it.

So what happens to it now?

Well, it has to be sent out in a form that's suitable for reproduction. And this is the responsibility of the production department. This sits within the agency's creative services department and is responsible for getting ads into newspapers and posters on to hoardings (hopefully that way round). They don't deal with TV or radio production.

This is the final stage in the creative process that began with a briefing and a blank sheet of paper and ends up with final artwork coming out of the studio.

The people responsible for making sure that the ads get to the right publications, at the right time – and to the right quality – are known as production controllers, and they work under the supervision of a production manager. (Some agencies call everyone in production a production manager, since they 'manage' their own particular clients, but the job function is still the same.)

At Poulter Partners, a large Leeds-based advertising agency, it is Lisa Lines who has this responsibility (although her actual title is Creative Services Director). She says, 'Production is the link in the agency that picks up the job after the creative work has been approved to progress to artwork. We co-ordinate the sending of the ad to the newspapers and this is mainly done electronically via **ISDN** lines using a system called "ADS". This is widely used by agencies. It creates an encapsulated file of the ad and sends it to the newspapers – then sends you back a sort of electronic receipt so you know it's been received safely.

'We work from the media schedule that shows when the various ads will be appearing, and what size they are, and work round our different copy deadlines on a week-by-week basis. We often clear about 150 ads per week to newspapers, consumer magazines and trade

titles.'

Alf Rogers is a production manager at JWT. He says, 'While an art director might be looking at a photograph from an artistic point of view, I'll be looking at it from a practical point of view and asking myself, will it reproduce well in the paper? I need to give the art director the best chance to get the best result.

'Some photographs might be too subtle to appear in newspapers, for example, where the **stock** is coarse. If I think there will be a problem, then I have to refer that problem back to the art director so he can decide what to do about it. We can check how an ad will appear by looking at the colour proof that comes in from the **repro house**. I'll show this to the art director and account handler for their comments. When they've approved it, I'll call the repro house and tell them to release it to the publication.

'At JWT we send out about a hundred different ads each week to the national press, local press and magazines. There's a lot of pressure put on us to get ads out faster. The media department leaves it until the last minute to book space so they can get the best prices.

Sometimes, the first I'll know about a new booking is when I get a call from one of the papers asking me to supply them with a particular ad – just minutes after the media department has booked the space.

'The problem is that with less time, you don't have the ability to think about the ads you're working on and try and anticipate any problems that might occur.'

The production controller needs to be an expert on photographic and print reproduction. Although most of what they do concerns press ads, in some agencies they might also be responsible for brochures, leaflets and all sorts of other print and display material. (In most large agencies these jobs would come under the remit of the print buyer.) In the case of posters, the production controller sends artwork to the poster printer and checks a colour proof in the same way he would for a press ad.

The production controller has to know what each newspaper or magazine requires in terms of material – can they accept the ad electronically or do they need **litho film**? They are responsible for making sure this material gets there before the copy date – this is the deadline when the ad (known as the 'copy') has to be at the newspaper. After that time they begin preparing the publication for printing; if the ad isn't there, the client will end up with a nice blank space.

(In reality this rarely happens but if they value continued employment, no production controller will take a chance. Imagine having to tell the account handler, 'I'm sorry that the ad didn't appear on the back page of the *Sunday Times* but I forgot to send it. And tell your client that I'm sorry he wasted £30,000 on the space.')

Production controllers are also responsible for the quality of the ad. Newspapers, magazines or repro houses will supply the agency with a colour proof which has to be approved and returned to them. The production controller must make any colour corrections to this or forever hold his peace.

It sounds straightforward enough. In fact it is, but the sheer volume of work and the constant pressure of deadlines (no to mention the constant threat of missing these deadlines) makes the job far from ordinary.

Lee Charles worked in the production department of DDB

and describes what he did on a typical day: 'The first thing was checking my schedules so I could see what ads I had to clear that day. If I was really efficient I would have already typed up my Copy Instructions. These are forms that are sent to the publications with the ads. They tell the newspaper or magazine who the client is, the name of the product the ad is promoting, the name of the publication, the date the ad is appearing, the size of the ad, the headline and, finally, what materials we are supplying. Sometimes it might not be obvious who the client is. There might not be a logo, for example, so they need this information to help identify it.

'These copy instructions – we call them CIs – are either delivered with the film that goes to the publications, or are faxed through in advance. We always make sure that we attach a copy of the ad to each CI we send. This is a sort of failsafe method to make sure the paper can recognise the ad.

'Sometimes we might release an ad to the newspaper and there might be a change to it, like a price has changed. Or someone's spotted a mistake. When this happens we supply the ad again – and it's even more vital that you attach a copy of the new ad to it. I always indicate what the change has been. It might be so small that you wouldn't notice it – this way we make sure that the paper knows.

'The traffic controller or sometimes the account handler will tell me when an ad is approved and I'll either get it sent over to the paper by ISDN or on a **Zip disk** or CD. Sometimes the photographic images will be separate transparencies that will need to be scanned in, but in most cases they would have already been scanned in and on the disk.

'I have to keep track of what's gone out and whether a colour proof has been received. The traffic man will take that proof around the agency, getting it approved. I'm ultimately responsible for the colour. I compare the proof to the original photograph on the **lightbox** and if it's needed, I'll ask the publication to make colour changes. It might be too warm or too cold, which means there's too much red or too much blue in the shot. If the colour is miles out then I'll ask for a re-proof. If the ad gets printed badly after I've seen a good proof then I'll take the matter up with the newspaper and try and get the client some form of compensation.

'We're always up against deadlines. If we're in danger of missing a copy date then I'll call the paper and try to get more time. They're usually quite good, as long as you don't keep doing it. Sometimes I can't get more time and I have to see if the media department can pull off a few favours through its contacts at the paper. With the amount of work we have going through it sometimes gets really hairy, though I haven't missed a deadline yet!'

Most people who work in the production department don't have formal qualifications. It's a department where, as long as you're bright, you can pick the job up as you go, gaining experience with everything you do.

Lisa says, 'Production is an area where many people join without any specific knowledge. I left college and worked at a photographic studio for a while. Then I joined a repro house. From there I worked at a mail order company and then switched to the agency side. At Poulters we had two production departments. One looked after the advertisements and one dealt with producing pro-motional items and display material, which is where I worked. I was then promoted to head up both departments.

'To work in the production department you've got to be very tenacious and very versatile. You've got to be good at multi-tasking as there are often ten, twenty or thirty jobs on the go at any one time – and you've got to keep all the balls in the air.

'What I like best is the variety. You don't know what you'll be doing each day. I love the pace and thrive on pressure. The downside is the long hours. I try and leave by six each night but ultimately, you have to stay until the job is done, and work around this anti-social lifestyle.'

In the production depart-ment, the entry-level position is production assistant, a job where you tend to help out the production controllers and managers by phoning around the newspapers, checking sizes for ads, specifications and copy dates. You'll also write copy instructions and do a fair amount of wrapping packages up and making sure artwork is delivered.

Within a year you should be able to look after your own accounts and take on the duties of a production controller. Some people are content to do this, working their way up to production manager, while others see it as a stepping stone to a job in traffic. To work as a production controller you need to be methodical and organised and, like most jobs in the advertising industry, be able to work under pressure. You should also have an interest in printing techniques and processes.

Before he joined JWT, Alf's background was in the print industry. Lee, on the other hand, joined as a production trainee after doing his A-levels. He says, 'I wanted to get into advertising and was lucky to get this job. I saw it advertised and went along for an interview. I was being shown round the production department when I bumped into someone I was at college with. We both studied art together and it turned out that he had joined a few weeks before me as a studio junior. I think he must have vouched for me, as the next day I got the job! I'm not sure what I want to do eventually but working in production gives you a good grounding and understanding of how ads are produced. I'd recommend it to anyone.'

GLOSSARY

● ISDN
A digital phone line that can transfer artwork and images at very high speed.

● Lightbox
A large illuminated screen where transparencies can be viewed easily, and compared with colour proofs.

● Litho film
Thin sheets of film that are used to make printing plates from which newspapers are printed.

● Repro houses
Companies that output litho film and colour proofs from artwork supplied to them. These films are made to the specifications required by the different publications.

● Stock
This is the technical term for the paper that magazines and newspapers are printed on. Newspapers have a very rough stock (called 'newsprint') while magazines have a much better quality paper. The better quality the paper, the better any photographic images will reproduce, and the finer the detail that will be visible.

● Zip disk
Proprietary type of floppy disk but with a much higher capacity, from 100 MB to 250 MB.

USEFUL SKILLS

Production controllers should be very systematic, neat and organised, with a good eye for detail and colour and a supreme sense of urgency. Accuracy however, is everything. Oh yes – and you'll need a sense of humour.

TIPS

● Write to the production manager or creative services director to see if there are any vacancies. Even offer to work for free just to get in.
● Read the section: **Other Routes into Advertising**.
● Some recruitment companies specialise in hiring production and traffic staff. See the back of *Campaign* for any vacancies.

COURSES AVAILABLE

The London School of Printing offers a short course, which while not totally relevant to the role of production controller, it provides a good background:
● **Appreciation of the Printing Processes (5 days)**
This course provides a basic technical knowledge and appreciation of the processes involved in print. Subjects covered include colour scanning and film proofing, paper selection, print finishing, binding, folding and digital printing.

For further details contact:

The London College of Printing
Elephant & Castle
LONDON SE1 6SB
TEL 020 7514 6770
WEBSITE www.lcp.linst.ac.uk

TRAFFIC CONTROLLER/ MANAGER

MONEY: £18,000 – £24,000 for traffic controller; £25,000 – £35,000+ for traffic manager.

HOURS: 8 – 10-hour days. Not that many late nights (except those when you're outside the pub bonding with the creative department).

HEALTH RISK: 3/10. Some creatives don't like being chased up by the traffic controller, but a scowl or the odd swear word are not life threatening.

PRESSURE RATING: 8/10. Can be pressured, especially if the job is overrunning at a number of different stages.

GLAMOUR RATING: 2/10. Sorry.

TRAVEL RATING: 1/10. Ditto.

The traffic department within an agency is responsible for co-ordinating the work flow (the traffic) within the agency, making sure that press ads meet their deadlines in time and on budget. Some traffic people are also responsible for allocating work within the creative department, ensuring that everyone's kept busy – and no one's overwhelmed with work.

The job's known by different names at different agencies. Other titles are 'progress chaser', 'traffic co-ordinator' or 'traffic man/woman'.

Think of all the different projects coming into an agency as cars (go on, humour us). Now think of the traffic man or woman as a policeman whose job it is to keep them moving smoothly. Like the policeman, the traffic man or woman has to be able to cope with cars that are moving too slow, cars that are travelling too fast, cars that are swerving out of control all over the place, and those which brake in the middle of the road, holding everyone else up.

Chris Watson has such a role at Poulter Partners. She says, 'My job is to plan in all the work and follow it through the agency. I make sure that the account handlers get the work when they need it and that the creatives all have enough work to keep them busy but not enough to swamp them.

'My involvement starts when I find out from account

handlers that work is coming in. I keep a database that contains a list of all the jobs in the agency. I use this every day and update it as and when I get new information. I keep a lot of what's going on in my head and tend to know what stages jobs are at because I'm familiar with them.

'We work to a timing plan structure which gives us dates when work is due at each stage, starting with an initial brief to creative right through to delivery to the client. I can chase work up according to where jobs are. If they're running late then I can try and reschedule them or get in freelance help to get them done. In consultation with the creative director I decide who works on what project. I know how suitable teams are for different projects and when I get the brief from the account handler, I can place the work accordingly.'

Cliff Carney is a freelance traffic man who works for a recruitment agency that specialises in providing temporary creative services staff. He says, 'Agencies take on people like me in between hiring permanent staff, for holiday cover or usually, to get them through a very busy period. I do pretty much the same things wherever I work.

'My main job is to make sure that the ads that are being produced are at the correct stage of development all the way from the time they're briefed to the creative team, to the time the final artwork is produced. From then on it becomes the job of the production controller to get the ads off to the newspapers or magazines – wherever they're appearing.

'Agencies are quite different when it comes to progressing work. Some are very sophisticated and have snazzy computerised timing plans that you can instantly update. Others use paper forms and some don't seem to have any real systems in place. Here it's down to the individual traffic person how they keep tabs on the workload!

'I get involved when the creative team are briefed first of all. I don't usually sit in on the meetings but I know from the account handler when the first designs are needed. This stage is called the 'internal review' and is when the account handlers see the first rough ideas. The next date is for finalising these and getting them mocked-up in a state where they can be shown to the client.

'My next key date is when photography has to take place. After this, it's retouching, then artwork. All the time I'm working back from the copy dates that have been given to me from the production department. These are the dates when the ad has to be sent to the publication. It's a fixed date and controls when every other stage needs to happen.

'I've got a desk but I'm hardly ever there. Most of the time I'm talking to people face to face whether it's the account handlers, the art buyer, the Mac operators or my production man. When I'm at my desk I'm normally compiling estimates, checking costs and that sort of thing.'

In addition to these duties, the traffic man is normally responsible for opening and looking after job bags. These are usually large A3 envelopes, one for each project. Each has a unique job number so that costs and orders can be allocated to it. In the bag go things like estimates, the timing plans, copies of layouts, photography, different drafts of copy, etc. – basically, anything associated with that job that you might need to refer to.

Budgeting is an important part of the traffic controller's remit. He or she has to collate costings for the job, present these to the account handlers and, when they're approved, keep track of them to make sure the budget is adhered to. If anything goes over budget – for example, retouching taking longer than anticipated – the traffic man has to keep the account handler informed.

Cliff likes the job because it gives him the chance to meet different people in the agency, and get involved in the creative process. 'Most creatives don't mind being chased up. I'll go into their office. Have a chat. Maybe have a cup of tea and see how things are going. It's quite casual. I'll have my timing plans with me and I'll check that they're aware of the deadlines – or that they know the deadline has come and gone! Some art directors or copywriters can be really precious about what they do and resent being gee'd-up. The copywriters are the worst, although most realise you're just doing your job!'

Jobs can overrun for all sorts of reasons. The account handler might have said that he needs two days for the client to OK the photography – but maybe the client's off sick, or away for a week. Then again, the creative team might be really struggling to come up with an idea and might need extra time. Anything like this has a knock-on effect on the whole job. In cases like this it's the traffic man's job to compensate for these problems; contracting deadlines here and there (or everywhere).

As for the sort of traits a good traffic man needs, Cliff says, 'Trafficking jobs is easy if you're organised and have a good memory. You have to be able to get on with everyone.'

Chris agrees, 'To be good as a traffic person you've got to be very, very organised. You've also got to be diplomatic since you're dealing with all sorts of people in the agency. You need to be able to prioritise work. You need to be able to say 'no' sometimes, and beg favours from people at other times. Making sure the work flows smoothly is all about keeping people informed.

'Poulter Partners is my first agency. I started out as a secretary for one of the partners but knew I wanted to do something more. I started helping out the traffic manager at the time and when he eventually left to become an account handler at another agency, I took over his job.

'As far as my typical day goes, it's normally a nine-to-five-thirty-ish job but you need to be flexible, and I'm sometimes in at weekends. It all depends on the workload and the nature of the work. The responsibility for making sure things happen when they should, rests with us. The account handlers might be late in getting a brief to us, but we still have to get the work done to the deadline given.'

Cliff started working in the production department at a large Manchester agency after taking his A-levels, but moved into traffic after three years. He's been doing the job for five years and began life as a temp about 18 months ago because of the variety it offered. He says, 'I like doing what I'm doing. I've got a good all-round picture of what goes on when you're creating an ad. I fancy being an art buyer and this experience is great for that sort of job.'

SKILLS YOU'LL NEED

To be a good traffic person you need to be methodical, have good people skills and the ability to be firm when needed. Since budgeting is an important part of your remit, you've also got to have a good head for figures. Thinking on your feet is essential, so you can work out the implications of a delay at any given stage in the job.

TIPS

● Most people join the traffic department after spending time in the production department (see the section on **Production Controller**).

● Read the section: **Other Routes into Advertising**.

● Some recruitment companies specialise in hiring production and traffic staff. See the back of *Campaign* for any vacancies.

TV PRODUCER AND PRODUCTION ASSISTANT

The agency TV producer is responsible for organising all aspects of the production of a TV commercial. Well, all aspects apart from actually filming and editing it, which are done by a film production company. As part of their job, they attend all commercial shoots wherever these take place, from Balham to Bali.

Advertising agencies don't actually make TV commercials. They create them, organise them and supervise them but the actual making – the filming and editing part – is undertaken by an independent film production company.

These are companies that provide a director and support staff who are responsible for the creative interpretation of the agency's script and then physically getting those images on film. (They will hire all the equipment and the crew from the cameraman, and the sound recordist right down to the gaffer and the best boy.)

The agency's TV producer is the link between the

production company and the agency. This is a vital role because of what's at stake: not just the money involved in filming a TV commercial (which can be from £100,000 to £750,000 or more – the British Airways commercial featuring all the famous people is reported to have cost just under £2 million) but also the repercussions if airtime is booked and the commercial isn't ready. With the airtime for a four-week campaign in and around London costing at least £1 million, the thought doesn't really bear thinking about!

Sarah Bales is a producer and also Head of TV at WCRS. She says, 'My main task is to budget and organise the production of TV commercials. Producers are the middlemen between the creatives, the account handlers, the client and the production company. It's an "all things to all men" type of job. My main task is to negotiate the budget on behalf of the client and agree costs for items that the agency is responsible for such as the actors, the music, post production facilities and editing.'

Working closely with the creative team who devised the commercial, the producer's first job is to help choose the director. Like artists, directors have different styles and abilities. If you were filming a new Nike commercial you probably wouldn't consider someone who directed a Shake 'n Vac commercial (and vice versa).

The creatives will probably have a view of who they would like to use because of work the director has done for other clients. Equally the producer, from his or her own experience, will probably recommend directors who are a) within the budget and b) suited for the type of commercial.

The TV producer would first request copies of the directors' **reels** and once a shortlist is made, send out scripts to a number of production companies to first of all, gauge their interest, then see if the commercial can be filmed within the time scale and, finally, to cost it.

The agency producer will then go through these budgets with a fine-tooth comb to see if costs can be saved here and there. For example, do we have to use a make-up artist at £2000 per day? Will the Georgian wigs really cost £4000? Do we really need to film it in Fiji when it's set in a fish and chip shop in Harrogate?

These savings might make the difference between being able to afford director A or director B. Alternatively, they might actually mean the difference between the commercial being viable or not (and no one likes telling clients that £500,000 is still not enough for the commercial that's just been presented to him – and which he likes).

Once the budget and a timetable have been agreed then the first stage of the commercial is 'pre-production'. Here the TV producer will work with the creative team and the production company in casting the actors and actresses, sourcing the soundtrack and considering the locations and/or set design.

After the commercial is filmed it goes into 'post-production'. Here the producer works with a facilities house on things like the editing, dubbing of special effects and music. Finally, they ensure that the commercial is approved by the BACC (the body responsible for making sure that commercials are legal, decent and honest) and that the tapes containing the commercial get to the right TV stations on the right dates. (Agencies are penalised for delivering the tapes too late,

which can cost them thousands of pounds. In addition, they must be up-to-date on technical requirements, for example, from 1 July this year, all commercials had to be supplied in wide-screen format.)

All through these processes the agency producer must keep a careful eye on the budget. A contingency is always built in but if bad light means that an extra day's filming is required, this can cost tens of thousands of pounds, particularly if you have to put up forty crew members in a hotel for an extra night and pay for an extra day's equipment hire.

The most vital attributes a TV producer must have are an eye for detail and an ability to keep cool in a crisis. Sarah says, 'As a producer you must demonstrate a willingness to do anything and pay great attention to detail. You have to be able to interpret people's views and deal with people at all levels. Diplomacy is vital since you often find yourself trying to make sure everyone involved in the project gets what they want.'

Sarah has been a TV producer for about eight years and loves what she's doing because it's so varied. 'The best part is the travel. I've been to

South Africa, America, Australia, Thailand, Spain and Prague. We end up filming in these sorts of places either because the creative idea requires it, because the weather is better, or because it's cheaper to film there. The job is quite pressured. There are some quite highly strung people involved and the hours can be gruelling. It's never a nine-to-five job, even in the office. We have to cram a lot in, in a short space of time since we're working to an air date that's immovable'.

Once you're a producer at an agency you can progress to Head of TV, with responsibilities for a number of producers and the overall quality of the service that an agency provides to its clients. Some agency producers decide to work for the production companies themselves. If you work with a busy director then you can earn a lot more money than you would at an agency, where salaries tend to be more or less level.

Then of course, there's the opportunity to start your very own film production company with a director. Who knows what the job could lead to...!

PRODUCTION ASSISTANT

Does attending TV shoots around the world and meeting the famous actors and actresses who appear in them sound glamorous? Of course it does.

Does getting into TV production at an agency sound difficult? Of course it does. But people do it by first getting their foot in the door by becoming a production assistant.

A production assistant and a producer work in regular teams, with the assistant doing the simpler tasks and more of the administration. As a production assistant you spend much more of your time in the office than going on shoots and sorting out a lot of issues 'behind the scenes'. Much of your time is spent on the phone liaising with the production company, arranging the casting sessions, sorting out licences and permissions for music usage, organising editing sessions, getting scripts approved, chasing estimates and invoices, updating budgets – that sort of thing. Basically, if you love administration then you'll love being a production assistant!

You can, of course, choose to stay a production assistant but most don't. They want to graduate to a producer after a couple of years, which is the natural career progression.

But how do you become a production assistant?

Well, there are two main routes. The first is getting a job in an agency in another department and making it known that you're interested in a career in TV. The reason many agency producers are female is that they've worked their way up from secretarial or PA jobs. (There's also the argument that women are better organisers than men, but the jury's still out on that one.)

Sarah says, 'I've hired people who've been receptionists, secretaries and even account handlers who want to work in TV. Qualifications aren't that important. Degrees in film production are helpful but not necessary. Commercial production has its own rules and what you've learned on a film course may not necessarily be relevant. It's more important to really want to work hard and show an interest in film production. Most people in the industry have learned through actually doing it.'

The other route into the industry is by starting as a runner at a production company, which is what Sarah did. She says, 'I took degrees in English and Drama but knew

people in advertising and that's what got me interested. As a runner I was basically a glorified messenger but you get to go on shoots and make contacts in the industry. You hear about vacancies as production assistants through word of mouth.'

Of course, there are hundreds and hundreds of people who want to be runners. What you need is grit and determination and to not be concerned that you end up doing the most menial of tasks for next to no money. Write to all the film production companies you can think of but better still, turn up on their door and ask if there's anything you can do. Anything.

RADIO PRODUCER

Hardly any agencies have specialist radio producers, the task being performed by the TV producers, or, more often, the production assistant. This is because radio production is far simpler, usually involving just the voice artists and the sound engineer at the studio.

A radio producer would primarily be involved with casting, budgeting and getting clearances, while the sound engineer would mix the commercial, adding effects and music as required.

GLOSSARY

● Airtime

Where, when and for how long the commercial will be shown. This is negotiated in advance with the different TV contractors by the agency's media department, or by an independent media consultancy.

● Reel

The director's show reel; a video compilation of his recent work that an agency can study to see if he/she is the right person for the job.

● Shoots

The filming of a commercial, which could last for a couple of days to a couple of weeks.

SKILLS YOU'LL NEED

To get into a TV department at an agency you'll need tenacity and the ability to stick at a 'lesser' job while biding your time for the right opportunity to come up. As a production assistant or a producer you have to be able to focus on separate jobs since you might have a few TV projects at various stages of development at any one time. Excellent organisational skills and attention to detail are critical, as is the ability to maintain budgets and monitor time-tables.

TIPS

● Get a foot in the door by applying for a secretarial/receptionist role but make sure the TV department knows you're interested in joining them.

● Apply to an agency for a work placement (write to the head of TV or the creative director).

● Subscribe to the trade magazines for production company professionals including *Broadcast*, *Televisual* and *Creative Review*. This will keep you informed about what directors and agencies are doing.

● Try to make as many contacts as possible in the industry, however tenuous.

● Learn to budget (runners get paid a pittance).

TYPOGRAPHER

The effectiveness and impact of an advertisement depends not just on the main image used, but on the style, size and colour of the typeface chosen – and how this is displayed.

These decisions are made by the typographer, who works closely with the art director or designer, although nowadays there is a blurring of responsibilities between what the art director, designer, artworker and typographer do. Read on...

To most people, many typefaces look alike and even an expert can have trouble differentiating between them. However, the choice of type is important in communicating the right message to the right audience.

Many characteristics of the product being advertised can be suggested or reinforced by the typefaces used. It goes without saying that you wouldn't use a flowery or feminine typeface in an army recruitment campaign. Nor would you advertise a ladies' razor using a typeface that wouldn't be out of place on a Motörhead album cover.

These are extremes but you can see how the typeface used in an advertisement is as important to conveying the right image and impression as the message itself.

Typographer Carlos Segura of the company T-26 says, 'Typography is beyond letters. Some fonts are so decorative, they almost become visuals and when put in text form, they tell a story beyond the words. A canvas is created by the personality of the collection of words on the page.'

But it's not just the selection of the typeface that's important. Typographers also have to give consideration to the **letter spacing** and **leading** in order to make sure the type is legible. They also have to bear in mind the end use of the item they are designing. For example, if it's an ad, will it appear in a newspaper or glossy magazine? If it's a brochure, then what will it look like? Considerations such as the texture and colour of the paper and the colour of the ink will also influence the effectiveness – or not – of a particular typeface.

As with most things, years ago life was simple. There weren't as many typefaces. Advertising was quite conservative and layouts were quite conventional. Most layouts followed the traditional, top down, 'headline, picture, copy' approach. In those dim, distant days most agencies had a typographer or two (usually called Jeff or Keith) whose job was to take a layout from the art director and specify the type in terms of the headline and the **body copy**. He or she would painstakingly trace over the layout by hand and draw in the headline to the right size and in the right style, then work out exactly how big the body copy should be and where it should start and finish.

This type specification was then sent out to a typesetting company who would deliver a **bromide** of all the text the next day (that's right, the next day). Someone in the studio would paste this down in position next to the relevant photographs in the ad, and if there was a change in copy, then another bromide would be ordered and stuck down. (You can see that the business wasn't so pressured then.)

It was a real craft and one of the old-school disciplines involved in the creative process with an apprenticeship system in place. These days, Macs have turned this profession completely on its head. Designers and art directors can see in an instant what their ad will look like when they change the style, size and even colour of different fonts.

But there are two other changes that have affected the way that today's typographers work.

Dingus Hussey is a typographer at BMP DDB and says, 'The principles of art directing are changing. Nowadays art directors are more concerned with developing concepts, and less with the final execution of their idea. They leave this to individual designers. That means there's more scope for designers and typographers to put their own "stamp" on the work.

'The second change is that the public at large becomes much more visually astute each year. They're more aware of type as a design element and are more sophisticated in their appreciation of what good typography sets out to achieve.'

With the growing awareness of type, designers have had to become far more fashion-conscious with regard to trends in design. Due to the quirky nature of the design business, typefaces and layouts fall in and out of favour. Typographers have to keep abreast of these trends and apart from reading magazines like *Creative Review* or *Design Week*, should read style magazines like *Wallpaper* or *ID*.

Often the style of the editorial will influence the style of the ads within the journal and there will be a sort of synergy between them. This gives the ads some extra kudos – it's as if the magazine has endorsed them.

Dingus got into typography after studying graphics at Great Yarmouth and Norwich College, where he got an HND and BA in Graphic Design. After graduating he took his portfolio round to loads of design companies and eventually got offered the post of junior designer. His advice is, 'Just see as many people as possible. Keep abreast of the latest fashions and trends. It's sometimes frightening how fast this industry moves. Also, try and make contacts with colleagues and suppliers in as many different companies as possible. When it comes to job opportunities it's amazing how important word-of-mouth is in this industry.'

So what makes a good typographer? Well apart from keeping up-to-date with trends, he or she has to have a real passion for type and see it as an art form in its own right.

They have to be able to appreciate what the ad is trying to do and who it's aimed at in order to make sure the type is sympathetic to these requirements. Being able to mimic a particular style is also very important. A particular design might try and pastiche a 60s psychedelic pop concert poster, a Wild West 'wanted' poster or an intricate Edwardian advertisement. In these examples the typographer would have to use a combination of his own knowledge and additional research to accurately parody the original imagery.

In some cases the correct font won't even exist and the typographer might have to design it himself from scratch.

Ostensibly, typographers are usually far more concerned with the quality of design of the final advertisement, brochure, packaging, etc. than whether the actual item will meet the client's objectives – either increasing sales or building awareness.

While this might seem blasphemous to the planner or account handler (and drive clients into apoplexy) it's not wrong. Ultimately typographers have to ensure that the message is communicated effectively – which should also mean that the client's objectives are met.

One typographer who has been in the business for more years than he would care to remember says, 'When I look at an ad I'm just looking at the blocks of type. I'm not looking at the ad as a whole but how these blocks look. Are they balanced correctly? Do they make a pleasing shape? Would they be better larger or smaller? If I can get this right then there's more chance of the ad being read, which has got to be the most important thing about it.'

GLOSSARY

● **Body copy**

The mass of descriptive text in an ad – i.e. not the headline or sub headings.

● **Bromide**

A sheet of thin photographic paper containing an image. In this case, the actual text that will be used in the artwork for an advertisement. Made largely redundant by the Mac.

● **Font**

Most people use this when they mean typeface, but a font is really the complete set of letters and symbols in a particular typeface. Virtually no one makes this distinction today.

● **Letter spacing**

The amount of space between individual letters, either to maximise readability or to fill a certain area. Adjusting the letter spacing is called kerning.

● **Leading**

This refers to the amount of space between separate lines.

There's no definite rule to follow. Sometimes too little space can be as bad as too much space.

● **Typeface**

The many different styles in which text on a page can be displayed. All typefaces have names. Common examples are Times New Roman or Helvetica. Most word processing programmes include a large number of different typefaces, which they call **Fonts**.

SKILLS YOU'LL NEED

A passion for type, a good sense of design and keen eyesight are pre-requisites for this job.

TIPS

● A graphic design course or degree is a good foundation for a career as a typographer, but most people take a job as a designer first to gain experience in an agency.

● Keep up-to-date with developments in typography by reading as many different style magazines as you can.

● Keep a portfolio of typography you like and add this to your portfolio of work created while you're studying (just never claim it's your own work).

USEFUL COURSES

The London College of Printing offers this highly relevant course:

● **Digital Typography (3 days or 6 evenings)**

This course is designed for anyone who wants to work in the fields of advertising and graphics who hasn't previously taken a formal typography course. Using an Apple Mac and QuarkXpress software, students consider a variety of typographic issues including page layouts, selecting fonts, examples of good and bad typography across a range of media, as well as the technical intricacies of copy fitting, kerning and line spacing.

These more general design courses are also available:

● Graphic Design: Introduction (4 weeks)

● Introduction to Professional Graphic Design (10 weeks)

● Graphic design for the Printed Page (10 weeks)

● Designing Promotional Material (3 days)

For further details contact:

The London College of Printing
Elephant & Castle
LONDON SE1 6SB
TEL 020 7514 6770

WEBSITE www.lcp.linst.ac.uk

● BA (Hons) in Graphic Design

A typical course includes a common first-year introduction to a wide range of design applications and ideas, followed by specialisation in design, illustration and (sometimes) advertising.

VISUALISER

MONEY: £25,000 – £35,000. Although a visualiser is not the highest paid employee in an advertising agency, a few companies do pay overtime which can make a huge difference. There's much more to be earned working on a freelance basis, or for an illustration studio.

HOURS: 9 a.m. – 6 p.m. approx. But given the vagaries of art directors' minds and the account handlers' propensity to brief everything at the last minute, be prepared for loads of late work (but possibly loads of overtime).

HEALTH RISK: 2/10. Well, how much danger is there when your main function is drawing? Even the posh felt pens called **magic markers** which most visualisers use are water based so there's little, if any, chance of ending up as a solvent abuser.

PRESSURE RATING: 8/10. Like nearly all jobs in advertising, you're working against the clock to get layouts and visuals finished for a presentation.

GLAMOUR RATING: 2/10 – 4/10. Sitting at a drawing board day in, day out, cannot, under any circumstance, be considered glamorous (well, unless the drawing board is diamond encrusted and you're seated on a throne – but that's highly unlikely). However, you might be drawing a **storyboard** for a fantastic TV commercial, in which case you'd be completely within your rights to say that you worked on that commercial…

TRAVEL RATING: 1/10 The only place you're likely to venture is to the local graphic art supply shop to stock up on magic markers and maybe the odd 2B pencil and rubber.

Despite the title, a visualiser isn't a creative guru whose job it is to conjure up great advertising campaigns as he sits cross-legged on the floor, eyes lightly closed, holding his fingertips to his temples.

No, it's a bit more down-to-earth than that – but it's a job that's vital to the 'selling' of a great idea.

The visualiser is someone who can illustrate, usually on paper, the concept that the creative team comes up with, whether it's a layout for a press ad, a poster or a storyboard for a TV commercial.

Video killed the radio star, and the **Apple Mac** killed the visualiser. Well almost. A long time ago, back in the days when *MacUser* only had eight readers, every agency had a visualiser. Or two. There they sat, perched high on their swivel stool in the studio, masters of all that they surveyed. Armed with an assortment of colour marker pens they would be able to make sense of an art director's senseless scrawl on the back of a beer mat and render it into glorious technicolour as a finished layout which a client could comprehend – or better still, approve.

With the advent of the Mac, visualisers went the way of the slide rule, carbon paper and tunes you could whistle. OK. That's an exaggeration. The Mac hasn't replaced the visualiser; it's just changed the work they're required to do.

These days, many press ads and posters can be mocked-up straight on screen using the Mac to manipulate images sourced from commercial **photo libraries**. But where visualisers are worth their weight in gold is in drawing separate frames for a storyboard and in the case of ads and posters, creating images that don't actually exist.

Say, for example, the agency wants to use Albert Einstein to endorse a new personal computer. And in this particular press advertisement, he's trying to peer in the floppy disc drive to see what makes the computer tick. At the end of the day, the agency would probably photograph an Einstein-lookalike, but for the purposes of the layout, someone would have to draw the scenario from scratch.

Here, the visualiser's skills lie not just in being able to execute the illustration convincingly, but in being able to match the art director or designer's brief. For example, should Einstein be smiling, crying, or looking puzzled? All of which would give the concept a completely different slant.

Ben Hasler is a visualiser at The White Room with five years' experience. 'The creatives come up with the original idea and my job is to put it in a form that can be shown to a client or put into research. Sometimes what we draw could end up as final artwork, like in the recent Guinness press ads. We do a lot of TV commercials here so I spend about 90% of my time drawing storyboards. At smaller agencies with less TV there's more of a balance between this and press ads or posters.'

So what makes the perfect visualiser? Well, apart from the obvious – being competent at drawing – you need to work fast.

It's no good creating a depiction of a Ford Mondeo leaping the Grand Canyon that's so good it actually looks like a photograph, if it takes two days to draw it. Successful visualisers know through experience what degree of finish they need to give a job to convey everything the art director wants – and when they're just embellishing an already good drawing for the sake of it.

Although most of the illustrations are drawn by hand, more and more visualisers are finding it quicker to colour them using the Mac, after first scanning them in.

Ben says, 'When I first started it took a long time for me to draw a scene. Now I can do it in about half an hour if I'm really pushed. I like having more time because I can put more thought into what I'm doing but sometimes being forced to work against the clock means you have to work more

loosely and this can actually look better.'

Visualisers with years of experience can draw most things from their heads. They know how someone or something looks like from any angle. Where the shadows fall. How the perspective looks. Most of the time though, the visualiser will be working from a reference. Over the years good visualisers will build up their own personal library of art text books, newspaper clippings, magazine articles, etc., that they take with them from agency to agency. The Internet, of course, is also an excellent resource. These references are also useful when it comes to mimicking different styles. For example, an art director might want a poster looking like a Warhol painting or something by Roy Lichtenstein.

When it comes to interpreting a brief you've been given, you should use your artistic skills and knowledge to advise the art director that changing the angle or the viewpoint might improve the idea. Most creatives are open to these suggestions.

What visualisers must not do is take it upon themselves to *change* the concept they've been briefed on. If the brief is to depict a hippo and a duck lying on a mattress together then there's a good chance that the art director wants this for a very particular reason – and not just as the result of some hallucinogenic substance.

Ben got into the industry by chance. 'After my A-levels I took a foundation course in art at the Kent Institute of Art and Design in Maidstone. I specialised in 3D art and actually wanted to go into animation. Until I could find the right job, I worked as a trainee insurance broker and absolutely hated it. I left this and did some work experience at a visualising studio where my cousin's boyfriend worked. Once I was here I was hooked. I knew it was something I really wanted to do.

'After the work experience ended I got a job as an office services assistant at an ad agency. My job basically consisted of photocopying and making tea and coffee. This was just as boring as selling insurance but I stuck it out, as it was a way of getting my foot in the door. While I was here I realised that hardly any of the art directors could draw. Some could do scribbles but that was it. I showed my portfolio to

some of the creatives and started getting freelance work from them. I then showed the work to the head of art buying, who also liked it. At the time, we were getting all our visuals done outside by freelancers. I was asked to write a proposal about setting up a facility in house and what savings doing it this way could make.

'The end result was that I set up the visualising department in the White Room. Although I still illustrate we get outside help on the larger jobs and one of my tasks now is to see freelancers and compile what's known as the WRIP – The White Room Illustrators Portfolio. We're putting this online soon so our creatives and TV producers can see at a glance who's on our books, with samples of their work. One of my other jobs is to manage these people in terms of checking the work against the brief and the time spent on it.'

Freelance or staff? Well, a freelance visualiser working for one of the large illustration studios or even one who's self-employed can earn a lot more money than someone who's employed by an agency. But you're more likely to get that elusive first job in an agency studio.

Ben offers this advice: 'The best way to become a visualiser is by knowing someone who's in the industry and getting the creatives to see samples of your work. If you can't do this then get a job as a dogsbody, make contacts and show your work. You'll get knockbacks but be determined.'

For Ben, it's the variety of work that makes his job so interesting. 'It's never the same thing any day. The people I work with are cool and there's a really good atmosphere'.

As for any downside, it's people changing their minds, right after he's finished an illustration. That and late nights. Ben says, 'It's OK now and then but sometimes I'll be working from say 8 a.m. to 2 a.m. the following morning to get something done. Then I'll have to be in at 8 a.m. the same morning to make sure everyone's happy with it. Some weeks I can be quiet and others I'm frantic. But when I'm quiet there's still things I can be doing, like researching new illustrators for our books and investigating new technology.

'All in all though I really enjoy it and it's a million miles away from insurance broking!'

GLOSSARY

● Apple Mac

In an advertising agency studio, Apple Macs are to computers as Magic Markers are to felt pens. The Macintosh computer was launched in the mid-80s and, because of the way it's designed, is very suitable for high-speed processing of graphic images. This means it's better than a PC for creating artwork, doing retouching – and even producing layouts for ads.

● Magic markers

Ubiquitous felt pen that virtually all visualisers use. Available in a huge array of colours (there are at least six different shades of grey, for example) and renowned for drying up just when you need that particular colour.

● Photo library

These are businesses offering commercial collections of photographs that ad agencies use either in mock-ups of ads – or, indeed, in the final ad itself.

● Storyboards

To present a TV commercial to a client the creative team will have devised a script. However, for it to be really convincing they will also probably show what's called a 'storyboard'. This is a collection of small drawings, each of which represents a key 'frame' from a TV commercial. Depending on how long and/or complicated the commercial is, the art director will decide how many frames are needed to convey the action – and what the content should be.

observe people wherever you are. On the train. In the park. In the pub. See how they sit or stand. How their clothes fold. Their expressions. That sort of thing.

SKILLS YOU'LL NEED
Visualisers need to have an inherent ability to draw and to work under pressure. A degree of neatness is also required.

TIPS
● If you can't get in to an agency, hand deliver a portfolio of your illustrations to the studio manager, creative director or head of art buying. Enclose a note saying you'll pick these up in a few days' time (it's actually better if you send them colour copies of your work and keep the originals safe).

● Take a finished ad from a magazine or newspaper and reproduce this as what might have been the original visual, both in black and white and colour. Include this in your portfolio.

● Set yourself a deadline. Work up your visuals to this deadline and keep practising to get your speed up.

● To improve your skills,